Lucio Casula

FACES, GESTURES AND PLACES

Pope Francis' Christology

LIBERIA EDITRICE VATICANA

Published in Australia by

© Copyright 2019 Coventry Press

Coventry Press
33 Scoresby Road
Bayswater Vic. 3153
Australia

Original title: *El Evangelio de la Misericorida en espiritu de discernimiento. La etica social del papa Francisco*

Translated into English by Salesians of Don Bosco of the Province of Mary Help of Christians of Australia and The Pacific

ISBN 9780987643186

© Copyright 2017 - Libreria Editrice Vaticana
00120 Città del Vaticano
Tel. 06.698.81032 - Fax 06.698.84716
commerciale.lev@spc.va

All rights reserved. Other than for the purposes and subject to the conditions prescribed under the *Copyright Act*, no part of this publication may be reproduced, stored in a retrieval system, or transmitted in any form or by any means, electronic, mechanical, photocopying, recording or otherwise, without the prior permission of the publisher.

Cataloguing-in-Publication entry is available from the National Library of Australia http:/catalogue.nla.gov.au/.

Printed in Australia

www.coventrypress.com.au

SERIES
THE THEOLOGY OF POPE FRANCIS

JURGEN WERBICK: *God's weakness for humankind.* Pope Francis' view of God

LUCIO CASULA: *Faces, gestures and places.* Pope Francis' Christology

PETER HÜNERMANN: *Human beings according to Christ today.* Pope Francis' Anthropology

ROBERTO REPOLE: *The dream of a gospel-inspired Church.* Pope Francis' Ecclesiology

CARLOS GALLI: *Christ, Mary, the Church and the peoples.* Pope Francis' Mariology

SANTIAGO MADRIGAL TERRAZAS: *'Unity Prevails over Conflict'.* Pope Francis' Ecumenism

ARISTIDE FUMAGALLI: *Journeying in love.* Pope Francis' Moral Theology

JUAN CARLOS SCANNONE: *The Gospel of Mercy in the spirit of discernment.* Pope Francis' Social Ethics

MARINELLA PERRONI: *Kerygma and prophecy.* Pope Francis' Biblical Hermeneutics

PIERO CODA: *'The Church is the Gospel'.* At the sources of Pope Francis' theology

MARKO IVAN RUPNIK: *According to the Spirit.* Spiritual theology on the move with Pope Francis' Church

ABBREVIATIONS

- AAS   *Acta Apostolicae Sedis*
- CCL   *Corpus Christianorum* (Series latina)
- DCE   *Deus Caritas Est*
- DV   *Dei Verbum*
- EG   *Evangelii Gaudium*
- EN   *Evangelii Nuntiandi*
- LF   *Lumen Fidei*
- LS   *Laudato Si'*
- MV   *Misericordiae Vultus*
- NMI   *Novo Millennio Ineunte*
- SE   *Spiritual Exercises*
- UR   *Unitatis Redintegratio*

PREFACE TO THE SERIES

From the time of his first appearance in St Peter's Square on the evening of his election, it was more than clear that Francis' pontificate would be adopting a new style. His modest apparel, calling himself the Bishop of Rome, asking the people to pray for him – in the 'deafening silence' of a packed square – and greeting them with a simple '*buonasera*' (good evening) … these were all eloquent signs of the fact that there was a change taking place in the way the Pope related to people, and thus in the 'language' used.

The gestures and words that have followed from that occasion only confirm and strengthen this first impression. Indeed, it could be said that over the ensuing years, the image of the papacy has been decidedly transformed, involving a change that affects homilies, addresses and documents promulgated as well.

As could be predicted, this has generated divergent opinions, especially regarding his teaching. While many have in fact welcomed his magisterium with enthusiasm and deep interest, sensing the fresh wind of the gospel, some others have approached it in a more detached way and, at times, with suspicion. There has been no lack of more absolute views, even going as far as to doubt the existence of a theology in Francis' teaching.

A summary judgement of this kind could come from the very different backgrounds of Francis and his predecessor, Benedict XVI. The latter, we know, has been one of the most outstanding and important theologians of the twentieth century and undoubtedly relied on his personal theological development in his rich papal magisterium. We have not yet fully appreciated, nor will we cease to appreciate, the depth of this magisterium. What Bergoglio has behind him, on the other hand, is his long and deep-rooted experience as a religious and a pastor.

However, this does not mean that his magisterium is without a theology. The fact that he was not mostly, or only, a 'professional' theologian does not mean that his magisterium is not supported by a theology. Were this the case, we could say that, strictly speaking, the majority of his predecessors were without a theology, given that Ratzinger represents the exception rather than the rule.

In any case, the fact that we can discuss the theological significance of Francis' magisterium, as well as the fact that, very often, some of his highly evocative and very immediate expressions have been so abused as to rob them of their profundity – in the journalistic as well as the ecclesial ambit – makes the response of this series, which I have the honour of presenting, a significant one.

By drawing on the competence and rigorous study of theologians of proven worth, coming from diverse contexts, the series has sought to research the theological thinking which supports the Pope's teaching. It explores its roots, its freshness, and its continuity with earlier magisterium.

The result can be found in the eleven volumes which make up this series with its simple and direct title: 'The Theology of Pope Francis'.

They can be read independently of one another, obviously; they have been written by individual authors independently of each other. Nevertheless, the hope is that a reading of the entire series would not only be a valuable aid for grasping the theology upon which Francis' teaching is based, in the various theological fields of knowledge, but also an introduction to the key points of his thinking and teaching overall.

The intention, then, is not one of 'apologetics', and even less so is it to add further voices to the many already speaking about the Pope. The aim is to try to see, and to help others to see, what theological thinking Francis bases himself on and expresses, in such a fresh way in his teaching.

Among the many discoveries the reader could make in reading these volumes, would certainly be that of observing how so much of the beneficial freshness of the Council's teaching flows into Francis' magisterium. This is true both of the theological preparation he has had, and of what has followed from it. Given that it is perhaps still too soon for all this wealth to become common patrimony, peacefully and fully received by everyone, it should be no surprise that the Pope's teaching is sometimes not immediately understood by everyone.

By the same token, a point of no return has been reached in Francis' teaching, one that recent theology and the Council have both taught: that doctrine cannot be something extraneous to so-called pastoral theology and ministry. The truth that the Church is called to watch over is the truth of Christ's gospel, which needs to be communicated to the women and men of every time and place. This is why the task of the ecclesial magisterium must also be one of favouring this communication of the gospel. Hence, theology can never be reduced to a dry, desk-bound exercise, disconnected from the life of the people of God and its mission. This mission is that the women and men of every age encounter the perennial and inexhaustible freshness of Jesus' gospel.

Over these years there have been those who have heard some of Francis' own critical statements regarding theology or theologians, and have concluded that he holds it and them in low esteem. Perhaps a more detailed study of the Pope's teaching, such as offered by this series, could also be helpful for showing that, while we always need to be critical of a theology that loses its vital connection to the living faith of the Church, it is also essential to have a theology which takes up the task of thinking critically about this very faith, and doing so with 'creative fidelity', so that it may continue to be proclaimed.

Francis' teaching is certainly not lacking in a theology of this kind; and a theology of the kind is certainly one much desired by a magisterium such as his, which so wants God's mercy to continue to touch the minds and hearts of the women and men of our time.

Editor-in-chief
ROBERTO REPOLE

CONTENTS

Abbreviations 4
Preface to the Series 5

CHAPTER 1

THE EPIPHANY OF MERCY 15

1. The 'Highest Revelation'............................. 15
2. The face of Mercy 19
3. The epiphany in history 30

CHAPTER 2

FLESH AND CROSS 35

1. The Incarnation 35
   1.1. The flesh of Christ............................37
   1.2. The fragility of the flesh 40
   1.3. The 'limited' Incarnation 42
   1.4. Incarnation and the Christian mission 44
2. Anointing 48
3. The cross 51
   3.1. Passion in the flesh............................51
   3.2. The failure of the flesh......................53
   3.3. Christian life as 'struggle'..................55
   3.4. The 'final battle' 60
   3.5. The hour of glory..............................62

Chapter 3

The Kerygma of life 67

    1. The primacy of Christ 68

        1.1. The almond blossom 69

        1.2. The personal encounter with Christ . 73

        1.3. The faces of others 76

    2. The 'Christological' option for the poor 80

    3. The 'formalitas Christi' 85

Chapter 4

A Work in Progress 91

    1. God's mercy and Christology 91

    2. A pneumatic Christology 97

    3. An incarnate Christology 100

INTRODUCTION

Why be interested in Pope Francis' Christology? He has not published any theological treatise on the mystery of Christ and salvation. Moreover, there is a widespread view that he is not particularly interested in theology, and he has been criticized, at times quite harshly, for showing little theological depth and a lack of doctrinal substance. His whole attention would seem to be focused just on evangelization and Church reform.

Actually, what animates Pope Francis is in fact an essentially theological and Christological concern. What is evangelization if not the proclamation of Christ? And what is it that urges him to be committed to Church reform if not the desire to have a Church which holds more closely to the message and style of Jesus so that it can fulfil its mission more credibly and effectively?

Even simple reflection on these points can help to understand the importance of the Christological dimension that motivates all of Pope Francis' ministry, including his commitment to evangelization and Church reform. Fidelity to Christ is the fundamental core of his teaching and his entire apostolate.

A reflection of this kind will also allow us to clarify what his Christological interest is. His 'Christology' is not a theological treatise which has been systematically developed in any 'desk-bound' kind of fashion, nor is it to be studied that way (cf. *Evangelii Gaudium*, no. 133, *EG*).

At the heart of his spirituality, his theology and his pastoral activity there is no static doctrinal core, nor a 'package' of values to be guarded and protected. What is there is the person of Christ and the living experience of personal encounter with him in the Church and in history. First of all, there is Jesus Christ who is the ongoing source of the gospel's eternal novelty and whose richness and beauty are inexhaustible (cf. *EG*, no. 11).

It is clear that Christology is not a Jesuology nor even a 'Christography'. It is not a Jesuology because it is not just a study of items regarding Jesus' life-story and history. It is not a 'Christography': though the term could be used to say that Christology is not a knowledge of everything that has been written and said about Jesus Christ throughout history.

Christology, based on personal experience, is the attempt to express the faith that Jesus is the Christ, the Son of God made flesh, who died and then rose for the salvation of all humankind. It is the knowledge of Christ, enlightened by faith, which must sustain a Church which 'goes forth', and guide Christians to live with and in Him, that is, in love of God and neighbour, in welcoming the least and the poor, in looking after the sick and the marginalized, and in being committed to respect for and protection of creation.

We can understand that Christology is not by nature – and even less so for Pope Francis – a purely theoretical discipline claiming to tell about Christ and make him known only through the study of texts and dogma. By holding steadily to the truth of the historical and salvific content of Scripture formulated through dogmatic propositions, it should lead to a personal knowledge of Christ, encouraging encounter with Him and discipleship. Therefore, the Christology that Pope Francis prefers is not found wholly and exclusively in books but is written first of all in the faces, places and gestures of Christ and human beings. It can be read on the faces of the poor, in existential peripheries and in gestures of closeness to people who are suffering.

In harmony with the spirit of Pope Francis, this current contribution will highlight some of the content and aspects of his Christological outlook, taking his Apostolic Exhortation *Evangelii Gaudium* as the main point of reference since he himself offered it as the agenda-setting document for his ministry. But we will not neglect other documents from his magisterium, or significant expressions of his activity prior to his election as Bishop of Rome.

In presenting the issues proposed by the Pope, the choice has been not to do it from a 'desk-bound' perspective, dissecting texts in order to focus attention on the dogmatic value of the language and content regarding the person of Christ and his ministry. Instead we will approach the texts in such a way as to take up some of the topics he has most at heart, considering them in their context, their connections and implications, especially of a spiritual and pastoral kind. The aim is to offer the reader an opportunity to appreciate the human depth and spiritual wealth of Pope Francis, fed by a profound faith in Christ, the profession of which reveals consequences of huge importance for Christology and the way of doing theology.

CHAPTER 1
THE EPIPHANY OF MERCY

One of the more obvious themes characterizing the preaching, magisterium and ministry of Pope Francis is mercy. For him, the message of mercy is the heart of the gospel, revealed in its fullness in the mystery of Christ, and which the Church must continue to proclaim and testify to through the faith and life of every Christian.

1. The 'Highest Revelation'

Jesus Christ is the 'Revealer' of the Father. Having come at the fullness of time, he brought to fulfilment God's manifestation in the history of salvation. As Pope Francis puts it, 'Jesus Christ is the Revealer *par excellence* of the mystery of God'[1] the one who proclaimed the Father and made him known (cf. Jn 1:18), because he told the world what he had heard from the Father (cf. Jn 3:32; 8:26; 15:15).

The Pope emphasizes that Jesus, the Son of God who came into the world, was fully aware 'of his own mission

---

1 J M BERGOGLIO – POPE FRANCIS, *Aprite la mente al vostro cuore*, Bur Rizzoli, Milan 2014, 122. Published in English as *Open Mind, Faithful Heart: Reflections on Following Jesus*, The Crossroad Publishing Company (November 18, 2013). Page references will, however, refer to the Italian text.

as Revealer of the Father'.² This is demonstrated by the authority with which he spoke and the power with which he worked. These were such as to arouse wonder, bewilderment and even fear.³

Nevertheless, the divine authority he showed, despite it being a sign of power was also the reason for his rejection.⁴ The light of his revelation was rejected due to the manner of his proclamation, since it was different from the way that human wisdom had hoped for and imagined.⁵ Therefore Jesus addressed his proclamation and communicated his knowledge of the Father to humble beings (cf. Jn 14:21), poor fishermen (cf. Mt 5:3), and simple folk (cf. Mt 11:27; Jn 14:7-9; Lk 10:21-22). Jesus also passed on to them his joy, and through his joy, the glory of God.⁶

However, Jesus Christ is not only the revealer of the mystery of God. He is also 'the Highest Revelation of the Father'⁷ Pope Francis uses this expression to emphasize that all of history 'tends to Christ and flows into Him.'⁸ Here the Pope refers to Scripture, quoting the initial verses of the prologue to the Letter to the Hebrews: 'Long ago God spoke to our ancestors in many and various ways by the prophets, but in these last days he has spoken to us by a Son, whom he

---

2 *Ivi.*

3 In his meditation, Pope Francis quotes the following Gospel passages: Mk 1:22, 27-28; Mt 28:18; Lk 1:35.

4 Cf. Mt 21:42; Acts 4:14.

5 Cf. JM Bergoglio – Pope Francis, *Aprite le mente al vostro cuore cit., 123.*

6 Cf. *Ibidem*,123-125

7 *Ibidem, 125.*

8 *Ivi.*

appointed heir of all things, through whom he also created the worlds. He is the reflection of God's glory and the exact imprint of God's very being, and he sustains all things by his powerful word. When he had made purification for sins, he sat down at the right hand of the Majesty on high' (Heb 1:1-3).

The text of the Letter to the Hebrews presents Jesus Christ not only as subject and mediator of revelation, but also as the 'object' of God's manifestation. The Pope explains: 'God manifests Christ to us. God saves us "according to his own purpose and grace. This grace was given to us in Christ Jesus before the ages began, but it has now been revealed through the appearance of our Saviour Christ Jesus, who abolished death and brought life and immortality to light through the gospel" (2 Tim 1:9-10).'[9]

The Pope also explains Peter's beatitude (Blessed are you, Peter ... Mt 16:17) from this perspective, along with that of the first disciples who had seen, heard and touched the Word of life made flesh with their own hands (cf. 1 Jn 1:1; Jn 1:4): the 'beatitude is not due so much to the fact that they were able to physically see Christ, but to the fact that it was the Father who had revealed him to them (Mt 16:17; 1 Pt 1:12).'[10] We can understand, then, that Jesus Christ is not only the one who reveals the Father but he is also the one whom the Father reveals to human beings. He is both revealer and revealed.

---

9   *Ibidem*, 126.
10 *Ivi*.

Jesus Christ is the 'highest manifestation of the Father' because he is the greatest gift the Father has given to humankind, the gift of the manifestation of his love. In fact the Apostle John writes: 'God's love was revealed among us in this way: God sent his only Son into the world so that we might live through him' (1 Jn 4:9).[11]

Finally, Pope Francis does not forget to underline the Trinitarian dimension of the gift of Christ, given that 'the revelation of Christ is a gift of the Father and the work of the Holy Spirit and is communicated to whoever allows the Spirit to come into his soul (1 Cor 14:26, 30; Phil 3:15).'[12] Through his work Jesus opens a breach for the flood of mercy which, together with the Father and the Spirit, he wishes to pour out upon the earth.[13]

Just the same, the ultimate manifestation of Jesus Christ will be an eschatological event because it will take place 'beyond the present time.'[14] The day of the *parousia* will be the day of the ultimate manifestation, with the final revelation of God's glory.

In the light of these reflections, revelation is Christologically marked not only subjectively but also objectively: Christ is the 'subject' but also the 'object' of revelation. He is the revealer as well as the fundamental content of divine revelation.

11 Cf. *Ivi*.
12 *Ibidem, 126-127*.
13 Cf. Pope Francis, *Homily*, Chrism Mass, 24 March 2016.
14 JM Bergoglio – Pope Francis, *Aprite la mente al vostro cuore, cit., 127*.

Furthermore, for the same reason it seems clear that revelation in Christ has both a theological and an anthropological value, insofar as it reveals the mystery of God and his purpose for humankind.[15]

2. The face of Mercy

Mercy, while being a fundamental theme of the biblical message and a central truth of the Christian faith, has been long overlooked by theology and philosophy, and relegated to the sidelines, confined to the area of morals and justice.[16] In continuity with his immediate predecessors,[17]

---

15 Pope Francis has in mind the content of the final document from Aparecida; cf. FIFTH GENERAL CONFERENCE OF THE EPISCOPATE OF LATIN AMERICA AND THE CARIBBEAN, *Aparecida Document. Disciples and missionaries of Jesus Christ so that we may have life in him*, 31 May 2007, no. 6: "Above all, we have been given Jesus Christ, the fullness of God's Revelation, a priceless treasure, the "precious pearl" (cf. Mt 13: 45-46), the Word of God made flesh, Way, Truth and Life of men and women, to whom he opens a destiny of utter justice and happiness. He is the sole Liberator and Saviour, who with his death and resurrection broke the oppressive chains of sin and death, and who reveals the merciful Love of the Father, and the vocation, dignity, and destiny of the human person."

16 Cf. W KASPER, *Mercy. The Essence of the Gospel and the Key to Christian Life,* Paulist Press (April 16, 2014), though here the reference is to the Italian edition, *Misericordia. Concetto fondamentale del vangelo – Chiave della vita cristiana*, Queriniana, Brescia 2013, 7-36.

17 We recall in particular John Paul II who dedicated his Encyclical *Dives in Misericordia* to mercy, 30 November 1980, in AAS 72 (1980) 1177-1232. The Polish Pope wrote in this encyclical: "I wish them to be a heartfelt appeal by the Church to mercy, which humanity and the modern world need so much. And they need mercy even though they often do not realize it" (no. 2);

Pope Francis has, commendably, brought it to the centre of theological attention and the Church's life, and has taken it up as a key term in his pontificate, right from the beginning of his ministry.[18]

On 7 April 2013, Divine Mercy Sunday, he began his ministry as the Bishop of Rome in the Basilica of St John Lateran by speaking of the experience of mercy which the Apostle Thomas had, and inviting us to always trust in God's mercy revealed in Christ.[19]

In him, as the very word '*misericordia* (mercy)' says ('*miseria*', wretchedness and '*cor*', heart), we see God's capacity for looking upon the wretched and human misery: in him we see God's ability to show compassion and to look after the poor and those in need of being liberated.

Interpreting Pope Francis' words and sentiments, Cardinal Walter Kasper explains: 'The statement: "God is mercy" means that God has a heart for the wretched. He is not a God in the clouds, so to speak, uninterested in the destiny of humankind, but rather does he allow himself to be moved and touched by human misery. He is a compassionate God, a "sympathetic" God (in the original sense of this word).'[20]

---

and again: "The genuine face of mercy has to be ever revealed anew. In spite of many prejudices, mercy seems particularly necessary for our times" (no. 6).

18 Cf. W KASPER, *La sfida della misericordia*, Qiqajon, Magnano (BI) 2015, 17-22.

19 Cf. POPE FRANCIS, *Homily*, Mass for the installation of the Bishop of Rome on the *Cathedra Romana*, Basilica of St John Lateran, 7 April 2013.

20 W KASPER, *La sfida della misericordia*, cit., 39.

In this regard, in order to better understand the terms of God's mercy, it could be useful to also add a detail offered by Cardinal Kasper regarding divine compassion: 'God is not touched by evil in a passive sense; in this sense there is neither passion nor suffering in God. Due to his absolute perfection, God is not moved, but due to his sovereignty in charity in an active and free sense, he allows himself to be moved and touched by human misery. There is no passion, but there is compassion in God.'[21]

Scripture reveals that God, 'who is rich in mercy' (cf. Eph 2:4), in order to save all of humanity in its misery, has taken this misery upon himself as if it was his, through the Incarnation of his Son. Thus the Incarnation of the Son of God has become a fundamental event of mercy. This is the first work of God's merciful love which took place in Jesus Christ:[22] He is mercy made flesh. The greatest manifestation of mercy, then, is given through the Son of God becoming man, and in his person. Saint Augustine used say: 'What greater mercy towards the wretched could there be, than that which brought the Creator of heaven down from heaven, and arrayed the Maker of earth in an earthly body; which placed on the same mortal level with ourselves Him who continues coequal in the eternal existence of the father; which laid the form of a servant on the Lord of the world.'[23] In his mercy, God was not content with forgiving the sins of

---

21 *Ibidem*, 39-40.
22 Cf. W Kasper, *Misericordia. Concetto fondamentale del vangelo*, cit., 173. To explore the theme of mercy in Scripture, cf. also K Romanuk, *La misericordia nella Bibbia*, Àncora, Milan 1999.
23 St Augustine, *Sermo* 207, 1 (PL 38, 1043).

human beings, but took the human condition upon himself.

'Jesus Christ is the face of the Father's mercy.'[24] This is how Pope Francis begins the Bull of Indiction of the Extraordinary Jubilee of Mercy. The Pope explains in this document that the Father, having shown his mercy in many ways and on so many occasions throughout the history of salvation, has visibly revealed it 'in the fullness of time' (Gal 4:4) through Jesus of Nazareth, his Son born of the Virgin Mary. Then, making reference to Vatican II's Constitution on Divine Revelation, *Dei Verbum* (*DV*), he states: 'Jesus of Nazareth, by his words, his actions, and his entire person[25] reveals the mercy of God.'[26]

Once he has pointed to the pastoral and spiritual reasons for the Jubilee, and when it is to begin and how it will develop, the Pope then immediately focuses attention on the theological motivations for this jubilee celebration, especially its Christological dimension. In fact, it is only by fixing our gaze on Jesus and his 'merciful face' that it is possible to grasp the love of the Trinity which he has revealed in its fullness. He revealed God's compassionate love for sinners, the poor, the sick, the marginalized and all who suffer.[27] The Pope writes: 'Everything in him speaks of mercy. Nothing in him is devoid of compassion' and again: 'What moved Jesus in all of these situations was nothing

---

24 POPE FRANCIS, *Misericordiae Vultus* (*MV*). Bull of Indiction of the Extraordinary Jubilee of Mercy, Vatican City, 11 April 2015, no. 1. See also nos 24 and 25.
25 Cf. *DV*, no. 4.
26 *MV*, no. 1.
27 *Ibidem, no. 8*.

other than mercy, with which he read the hearts of those he encountered and responded to their deepest need.'[28] He also reminds us of the compassion Jesus showed to people who were weary, exhausted and who followed him around like sheep without a shepherd (cf. Mt 9:36); to the sick who were brought to him (cf. Mt 14:14); to the crowd who had followed him for three days and for whom he had multiplied the loaves and the fishes (cf. Mt 15:32-38); to the widow of Naim, whose only son he had brought back to life (cf. Lk 7:12-15); to the Gerasene demoniac whom he had freed from the 'Legion' of unclean spirits (cf. Mk 5:2-19).

In particular, the Pope recalls the episode of Matthew's call when Jesus 'looked upon Matthew with merciful love',[29] forgiving him his sins and calling him to become one of the Twelve.[30] Concerning this Gospel scene, and quoting St Bede the Venerable,[31] the Pope notes that 'Jesus looked upon Matthew with merciful love and chose him: *miserando atque eligendo*.[32]' Then he adds, confidentially, 'This expression

---

28 *Ivi.*
29 Pope Francis says that the secret to Jesus is hidden in his gaze (cf. *Evangelii Gaudium*, *EG*, no. 14): it is a gaze full of affection and concern for all his people (cf. *EG*, no. 268) and full of love and mercy for sinners (cf. *EG*, no. 269).
30 "This is what Jesus did and does with everyone, especially sinners and those excluded from society: he looked at them in such a way as to make them feel recognized in their dignity, and they were converted, healed, were welcomed and transformed into his disciples" JM BERGOGLIO, '*Dignity and fullness of life*', *Homily*, Feast of St Cajetan, 7 August 2007, in JM BERGOGLIO – POPE FRANCIS, *È amore che apre gli occhi*, Rizzoli, Milan 2013, 197.
31 BEDE THE VENERABLE, *Homily* 21.
32 "Vidit ergo publicanum et quia miserando atque eligendo

impressed me so much that I chose it for my episcopal motto.'[33]

The Pope has also presented any number of parables that reveal God's compassion, mercy and love, and that teach us how to live in a merciful way.[34] He writes: 'Jesus affirms that mercy is not only an action of the Father, it becomes a criterion for ascertaining who his true children are.'[35] With regard to this, Pope Francis draws attention to the parables of the lost sheep, the lost coin, the father and his two sons (cf. Lk 15:1-32) and the 'merciless servant', told to explain forgiveness offered seventy times seven (cf. Mt 18:21-35). 'Jesus is all mercy, Jesus is all love: he is God made man. Each of us, each one of us, is that little lost lamb, the coin that was mislaid; each one of us is that son who has squandered his freedom on false idols, illusions of happiness, and has lost everything. But God does not forget us, the Father never abandons us. He is a patient father, always waiting for us!'[36]

The complete manifestation of mercy, however, is in Jesus' cross, in the mystery of his death and resurrection. For Pope Francis, the crucifix is the concrete image of God's mercy: 'Good Friday is the culminating moment of love.

vidit *ait illi: Sequere me*" *(Homelia 21,55: CCL 122, 149-150).*

33 *MV,* no. 8.

34 Cf. THE PONTIFICAL COUNCIL FOR PROMOTION OF THE NEW EVANGELIZATION, *The Parables of Mercy,* Our Sunday Visitor Inc. US, 2105. Cf. W KASPER, *Misericordia. Concetto fondamentale del vangelo,* cit., 94-126. (English: *Mercy. The Essence of the Gospel and the Key to Christian Life).*

35 *MV,* no. 9.

36 POPE FRANCIS, *Angelus,* St Peter's Square, 15 September 2013.

The death of Jesus, who on the Cross surrenders himself to the Father in order to offer salvation to the entire world, expresses love given to the end, a love without end. A love that seeks to embrace everyone, that excludes no one. A love that extends over time and space: an inexhaustible source of salvation to which each of us, sinners, can draw.'[37] It is on the cross that 'the dramatic encounter of the sin of the world and God's mercy' (*EG*, no. 285) takes place. It is on Christ's cross that we see the full manifestation of the greatness and gratuitousness of God's love,[38] which is the origin of his 'compassion' for humankind.

---

37 POPE FRANCIS, *General Audience*, St Peter's Square, 23 March 2016. See also the following reflection: "Why the Cross? Because Jesus takes upon himself the evil, the filth, the sin of the world, including the sin of all of us, and he cleanses it, he cleanses it with his blood, with the mercy and the love of God" (*Homily*, Palm Sunday, 28th World Youth Day, St Peter's Square, 24 March 2103).

38 "God placed on Jesus' Cross all the weight of our sins, all the injustices perpetrated by every Cain against his brother, all the bitterness of the betrayal by Judas and by Peter, all the vanity of tyrants, all the arrogance of false friends. It was a heavy Cross, like night experienced by abandoned people, heavy like the death of loved ones, heavy because it carries all the ugliness of evil. However, the Cross is also glorious like the dawn after a long night, for it represents all the love of God, which is greater than our iniquities and our betrayals. In the Cross we see the monstrosity of man, when he allows evil to guide him; but we also see the immensity of the mercy of God, who does not treat us according to our sins but according to his mercy. Before the Cross of Jesus, we apprehend in a way that we can almost touch with our hands how much we are eternally loved; before the Cross we feel that we are "children" and not "things" or "objects", as St Gregory of Nazianzus says, addressing Christ ..." (POPE FRANCIS, *Address*, Via Crucis at the Colosseum, Good Friday, 18 April 2014).

At the summit of the revelation of the mystery of God is the paschal mystery of Christ that represents the definitive victory of mercy over human wretchedness. In his resurrection, Christ, having accepted the cross, fully reveals the God of compassion and merciful love who is more powerful than evil and death. Victorious over sin and death, Christ continues to act in the present, sowing seeds of new life everywhere: 'Christ's resurrection everywhere calls forth seeds of that new world; even if they are cut back, they grow again, for the resurrection is already secretly woven into the fabric of this history, for Jesus did not rise in vain' (*EG*, no. 278). In the light of the paschal mystery, then, Christ appears as the ultimate incarnation of mercy and its historical, salvific and eschatological living sign.[39] Mercy is not simply a divine attribute or property but is the essence itself of God's love shown through Jesus Christ. For Pope Francis, mercy is 'the beating heart of the Gospel'[40] that wells up and overflows unceasingly like a great river from the deepest recesses of the divine mystery, from the heart of the Trinity.[41]

In his Apostolic Exhortation *EG*, while explaining that there is a 'hierarchy' of the truths of faith in Catholic doctrine, due to their capacity for expressing the core of the gospel, the Pope writes that the basic core is '*the beauty of the saving love of God made manifest in Jesus Christ who died*

---

39 Cf. POPE JOHN PAUL II, *Dives in Misericordia*, no. 8.
40 *MV*, no. 12.
41 Cf. *Ibidem*, no. 25.

and rose from the dead[42] (*EG*, no. 36). Then, concerning the Church's moral teachings, also subject to this 'hierarchy' of truths, quoting St Thomas Aquinas[43] the Pope says that mercy is the greatest of all the virtues (cf. *EG*, no. 37).

These themes also return in the Apostolic Letter *Misericordia et Misera*, written at the end of the Jubilee,[44] where he calls on the especially effective Gospel icon of the encounter between Jesus and the woman taken in adultery (cf. Jn 8:1-11). Taking his cue from St Augustine's commentary on this, the Pope shows how 'all is revealed' and 'all is resolved' in mercy that is shown concretely in the encounter with Jesus: 'A woman and Jesus meet. She is an adulteress and, in the eyes of the Law, liable to be stoned. Jesus, through his preaching and the total gift of himself that would lead him to the Cross, returned the Mosaic Law to its true and original intent. What is central here is not the law or legal justice but the love of God, which is capable of looking into the heart of each person and seeing the deepest desire hidden there; God's love must take primacy over all else. This Gospel account, however, is not an encounter of

---

42 The italics are in the Pope's text.

43 The text he quotes is as follows: "In itself mercy is the greatest of the virtues, since all the others revolve around it and, more than this, it makes up for their deficiencies. This is particular to the superior virtue, and as such it is proper to God to have mercy, through which his omnipotence is manifested to the greatest degree" (*Summa Theologiae*, II-II, q. 30, art. 4). He then adds a further text from St Thomas Aquinas in a note: *Summa Theologia*, II-II, q. 30, art. 4, ad 1.

44 Cf. POPE FRANCIS, *Misericordia et Misera*, *Apostolic Letter at the conclusion of the Extraordinary Jubilee of Mercy*, Vatican City, 20 November 2016.

sin and judgement in the abstract, but of a sinner and her Saviour. Jesus looked that woman in the eye and read in her heart a desire to be understood, forgiven and set free. The misery of sin was clothed with the mercy of love.'[45] At the heart of the mystery of compassion and mercy, there is always Jesus Christ: in him is shown the primacy of God's love for the sinful human being in need of help.

In the first Encyclical signed by Pope Francis, *Lumen Fidei* (*LF*),[46] the first draft of which had been prepared by Pope Benedict XVI, we read: 'At the heart of biblical faith is God's love, his concrete concern for every person, and his plan of salvation which embraces all of humanity and all creation, culminating in the Incarnation, death and resurrection of Jesus Christ' (*LF*, no. 54).

At this point it is important to emphasize once more the theological and Christological import of mercy. By placing mercy at the heart of the faith and Christian and ecclesial life, the Pope is offering an opportunity to reflect on the fundamental content of the biblical message and God's revelation in Christ, but also for better understanding the Christian novelty, the value of Incarnation and human beings' relationship with God. In fact Christ's Incarnation, by comparison with earlier philosophical and religious traditions, brought about a radical reversal of the relationship between human beings and God, and the logic of salvation.[47]

45 *Ibidem*, no. 1.
46 POPE FRANCIS, *Lumen Fidei*, Encyclical, 29 June 2013.
47 Cf. R CANTALAMESSA, *Il volto della misericordia, Piccolo trattato sulla divina e sulla umana misericordia*, San Paolo, Cinbisello Balsamo (MI) 2015, 25-28.

From the Christian perspective, salvation is not won through a difficult ascetical journey toward God and divine realities which is taken up through human initiative. The Christian novelty is that the Word became flesh and took upon himself the human condition. So, it is not the human being who takes the initiative to go toward God, but God who has taken the initiative and, out of his compassion and mercy, through the Incarnation of his Son, has come down to human beings.[48] Clearly the motivation behind such a 'reversal' concerning God and humankind in Christ is love, that is, mercy. St John has written: 'In this is love, not that we loved God but that he loved us and sent his Son to be the atoning sacrifice for our sins ...We love because he first loved us' (1 Jn 4:10. 19).

We also find in the Apostolic Exhortation *EG* that God's love manifested in Jesus Christ is the source of all human joy (cf. *EG*, no. 7). Pope Francis states that the core

---

48 "We may derive two considerations from the joyous contemplation of the mystery of the Son of God born for us. The first is that if God, in the Christmas mystery, reveals himself not as One who remains on high and dominates the universe, but as the One who bends down, descends to the little and poor earth, it means that, to be like him, we should not put ourselves above others, but indeed lower ourselves, place ourselves at the service of others, become small with the small and poor with the poor ... The second consequence: if God, through Jesus, involved himself with man to the point of becoming one of us, it means that whatever we have done to a brother or a sister we have done to him. Jesus himself reminded us of this: whoever has fed, welcomed, visited, loved one of the least and poorest of men, will have done it to the Son of God" (POPE FRANCIS, *General Audience*, St Peter's Square, 18 December 2013).

and essence of the Christian proclamation is 'the God who revealed his immense love in the crucified and risen Christ', the 'eternal Gospel' (Rev 14:6), the one who is 'the same yesterday, today and forever' (Heb 13:8), whose riches and beauty are inexhaustible (*EG*, no. 11). In fact, Jesus Christ is able to break through the tiresome schemes within which human beings try to imprison him, and can surprise us with his divine creativity.

We are talking about a topic that was already presented in a homily at Mass celebrated by Cardinal Bergoglio in October 2002[49] for the third Congress of Communicators. Referring to the Good Samaritan, he spoke of the beauty of love: 'In Jesus who died on the cross, which has no semblance to nor a "presence" of any kind to offer the eyes of the world or television cameras, the beauty of the marvellous love of a God who gives his life for us shines through. It is the beauty of charity, the beauty of the saints.'[50] The beauty of God's love is alive in Jesus Christ who died and was risen and in his merciful presence to humankind.

3. *The epiphany in history*

For the Church and all Christians, the task of opening their hearts and being compassionate in the precarious and suffering circumstances afflicting the world flows from the

---

[49] *Comunicatore, chi è il tuo prossimo?*, *Homily*, 3rd Congress of Communicators, October 2002, in JM BERGOGLIO – POPE FRANCIS, *È l'amore che apre gli occhi,* cit., 112-122.

[50] *Ibidem,* 119.

Christological basis of the manifestation of God's love and mercy.

In the Bull of Indication for the Jubilee, referring to the scene of the last judgement, based on the attitude to the hungry, thirsty, strangers, the naked, sick or in prison, (cf. Mt 25:31-46), Pope Francis recommends practising the corporal[51] and spiritual[52] works of mercy. He writes: 'In each of these "little ones," Christ himself is present. His flesh becomes visible in the flesh of the tortured, the crushed, the scourged, the malnourished, and the exiled… to be acknowledged, touched, and cared for by us'[53]

Then, commenting on the account of Jesus' visit to the synagogue in Nazareth (cf. Lk 4:16-21), when he got up to read the passage from the Prophet Isaiah about his mission: 'The spirit of the Lord God is upon me, because the Lord has anointed me; he has sent me to bring good news to the oppressed, to bind up the brokenhearted, to proclaim liberty to the captives, and release to the prisoners; to proclaim the year of the Lord's favour' (Is 61:1-2), the Pope explains the Christian's task 'to bring a word and gesture of consolation to the poor, to proclaim liberty to those bound by new forms of slavery in modern society, to restore sight to those who

---

51 The seven corporal works of mercy are: feeding the hungry, giving the thirsty to drink, clothing the naked, welcoming strangers, visiting the sick, visiting prisoners and burying the dead.

52 The seven works of spiritual mercy are: teaching the ignorant, advising the doubtful, consoling the afflicted, correcting sinners, forgiving offences, patiently putting up with those who wrong us and praying to God for the living and the dead.

53 *MV*, no. 15.

can see no more because they are caught up in themselves, to restore dignity to all those from whom it has been robbed. The preaching of Jesus is made visible once more in the response of faith which Christians are called to offer by their witness.'[54]

Cardinal Kasper notes that for Pope Francis, mercy is not just a social or ecclesial virtue, but has a Christological and mystical dimension with roots in the Bible and patristic tradition. He writes: 'Jesus came to preach the gospel, good news for the poor (cf. Lk 4:18); he who was rich, abased himself and became poor and weak to the extent of the cross (cf. 2 Cor 8:9). This *kenosis*, this self-abasement, this self-spoliation and self-humiliation continues in his mystical body which is the Church, continues in the poor. Pope Francis often says that we can touch Jesus in the sores of the wounded and the poor; what we have done for the poor and the wretched we have done to him (cf. Mt 25:40).'[55]

So, the Pope presents mercy as a 'fundamental aspect of Jesus' mission' but also maintains 'the primacy of mercy' as the rule of the disciples' life[56] and the rule for the entire Church. In *EG* he writes: 'The Church must be a place of mercy freely given, where everyone can feel welcomed, loved, forgiven and encouraged to live the good life of the Gospel' (*EG*, no. 114).

The Church's primary task 'is to introduce everyone to the great mystery of God's mercy by contemplating the face

---

54 *Ibidem*, no. 16.
55 W KASPER, *La sfida della misericordia*, cit., 55.
56 *MV*, no. 20.

of Christ. The Church is called above all to be a credible witness to mercy, professing it and living it as the core of the revelation of Jesus Christ.'[57]

'The epiphany of God in Christ, the revelation of his gift, does not end with Jesus' earthly existence: it will continue to be passed on "from faith to faith", over history, thanks to men and women who, having accepted him in their lives, become disciples and apostles for others.'[58] This thought sustains the image of Christ as the one who reveals God in his earthly existence, but it also insists on the fact that revelation continues thanks to men and women who have accepted and welcomed Christ's revelation.[59] Here we can see the Christological dimension of revelation given through Jesus' life and words but also in the transmission of faith of all those who share in the mystery of Christ and 'become disciples and apostles for others.' What St Paul writes about himself, 'He was pleased to reveal his Son to me' (Gal 1:15-16) applies equally to all men and women who become disciples and apostles.

Pope Francis states: 'We receive the mission as apostles (Rom 1:5) from Christ himself who reveals himself to us, and it is the same Christ who speaks and acts through us (Rom 15:18), who is not weak but powerful, thanks to the preaching that is born within us when we have accepted his

---

57 *Ibidem*, no. 25.
58 JM BERGOGLIO – POPE FRANCIS, *Aprite la mente al vostro cuore*, cit., 118.
59 The Pope quotes the following New Testament texts: 2 Tim 1:5; Gal 1:15-16; Jn 21:1; 1 Cor 9:1; 15:8; 15:11; Eph 3:5 and Rom 16:25-27.

manifestation (2 Cor 13:3).'[60] Jesus reveals to humankind, but also in and through humankind. So, disciples of every age who heed others are heeding Jesus himself.

We can say that God's revelation always takes place in the manner of the Incarnation; or in other words, God's revelation that took place through the Incarnation of the Son continues to happen in the flesh of men and women of every age. Pope Francis says: 'God's epiphany, accepted in us, becomes flesh in the life of the disciple, such that it can be passed on only through this "Incarnation", so not through words of flesh and blood, nor thanks to human wisdom, but through the scandal of, the need for the cross: it can be passed on only by *martyrion*, by witness.'[61]

God's revelation continues to be transmitted only through his 'incarnation' in the life of his disciples and of every Christian who bears testimony to Christ through his or her life, as far as the cross.

---

60 JM BERGOGLIO – POPE FRANCIS, *Aprite la mente al vostro cuore*, cit., 119.

61 *Ibidem*, 119-120.

Chapter 2
FLESH AND CROSS

Flesh and cross represent the two basic moments of the mystery of Christ: the Incarnation and Easter, or the two poles within which the mission of the Son of God, who came into the world for the salvation of humankind, is accomplished. All of Christ's earthly existence turns around the Incarnation and Easter.

Flesh and cross are also the essential components for the reality and authenticity of the Incarnation. The Christian faith is founded on the Son of God made flesh and on the physical reality of the person of Christ and his history. In contrast to those who 'want a purely spiritual Christ, without flesh and without the cross' (*Evangelii Gaudium*, no. 88, *EG*), authentic Christian faith focuses on the truth of the Incarnation of the Son of God and on the truth of his flesh and cross.

'Flesh' and 'cross', then, in Pope Francis' reflections, are strongly relevant at the theological, spiritual and pastoral level. They are the coordinates which allow us to understand the identity of the person of Christ and his mission, as well as the Christian mission and vocation.

1. The Incarnation

Christ, the divine Word through whom all things were created, became flesh (Jn 1:14). In his Encyclical *Laudato Si'*

(*LS*), Pope Francis writes: 'One Person of the Trinity entered into the created cosmos, throwing in his lot with it, even to the cross. From the beginning of the world, but particularly through the Incarnation, the mystery of Christ is at work in a hidden manner in the natural world as a whole, without thereby impinging on its autonomy' (*LS*, no. 99).

Jesus Christ is the Incarnation of the living God and the one who brings human beings God's life. It is he who, faced with death, sin and selfishness, accepts, loves, forgives and gives back life.[1]

In the mystery of the Incarnation the Pope contemplates the coming of the Lord into the world and the fact that 'though He is the Creator, He has stooped to become man'[2] and, born in poverty, after going through all kinds of suffering, died on the cross.[3]

Jesus' birth shows that God has taken the side of human beings once and for all in order to raise them up from wretchedness and sin.[4] In a reflection on religious life entitled 'Be custodians of your legacy',[5] Bergoglio wrote: '... The God of our Jesuit legacy will be the *God incarnate*: Jesus

---

1 Cf. POPE FRANCIS, *Homily*, Mass for "Evangelium Vitae" Day, St Peter's Square, 16 June 2013.

2 IGNATIUS OF LOYOLA, *Spiritual Exercises*, no. 53. (taken from the English translation by Louis J Puhl, SJ).

3 Cf. *Ibidem*, no. 116.

4 Cf. POPE FRANCIS, *General audience*, 18 December 2013.

5 Cf. JM BERGOGLIO – POPE FRANCIS, *Nel cuore di ogni padre. Alle radici della mia spiritualità*, Bur Rizzoli, Milan 2016, 26-34. Written by Bergoglio in 1982, the volume brings together meditations and written material of a mainly spiritual nature which reveal the Ignatian and Jesuit roots of his thinking and spirituality.

Christ, our Lord, who companion we are by vocation. God has planted his tent in our midst (cf. Jn 1:14 …) and became "one of us". It is not only Jesus' death and resurrection that saves us and calls us, as one could infer from a reductionist christology, the very person of Jesus: the Lord who takes flesh, is born, cares for, teaches, suffers, dies, rises, remains among us.'[6]

1.1 The flesh of Christ

In becoming man, the Son of God became fully a part of human life: by taking on flesh he also took on 'culture, way of being, categories of thought, language, values, history …'[7] God's presence among human beings did not happen in any ideal or idyllic way but in the real world marked by many divisions, wickedness, poverty, arrogance, violence and war.

In the Incarnation of his Son, God wanted to share the human condition to the point of becoming one with human beings in the person of Jesus, true man and true God.[8] He became man 'in earnest' and 'in earnest' has taken up the mission assigned to him by his Father, bringing it to completion with humility, to the point of 'self-annihilation'.

In the cathedral at Cagliari, speaking to the poor and to prison inmates, Pope Francis said: 'Looking at Jesus we see he chose the path of humility and service. Rather, he himself is this path. Jesus was not indecisive; he was not indifferent. He made a decision and followed it through

6   Cf. *Ibidem*, 29.
7   *Ibidem*, 257.
8   Cf. POPE FRANCIS, *General audience*, 18 December 2013.

until the end. He decided to become man and as a man to become a servant until his death on the Cross. This is the way of love, there is no other."[9]

Jesus' manner of being and lifestyle can be fully represented with the categories of humility and service unto death.[10] His story, in fact, was not the fulfilment of a destiny suffered passively, but a path of confident entrustment and voluntary surrender in response to the love of the Father.[11] Christ came into the world to do God's will and his sacrifice became a reason for justification and salvation.[12]

---

9 POPE FRANCIS, *Address to the poor and prison inmates*, Cagliari, 22 September 2013.

10 "These words show us God's way and, consequently, that which must be the way of Christians: it is humility. A way which constantly amazes and disturbs us: we will never get used to a humble God! Humility is above all God's way: God humbles himself to walk with his people, to put up with their infidelity ... This is God's way, the way of humility. It is the way of Jesus; there is no other. And there can be no humility without humiliation. Following this path to the full, the Son of God took on the "form of a slave" (cf. Phil 2:7). In the end, humility also means service. It means making room for God by stripping oneself, "emptying oneself", as Scripture says (v. 7). This – the pouring out of oneself – is the greatest humiliation of all" (POPE FRANCIS, *Homily*, Palm Sunday, 30th World Youth Day, St Peter's Square, 29 March 2015).

11 "Jesus does not experience this love that leads to his sacrifice passively or as a fatal destiny. He does not of course conceal his deep human distress as he faces a violent death, but with absolute trust commends himself to the Father. Jesus gave himself up to death voluntarily in order to reciprocate the love of God the Father, in perfect union with his will, to demonstrate his love for us" (POPE FRANCIS, *General Audience*, 27 March 2013)

12 Cf. POPE FRANCIS, *Homily*, Mass at Domus Sanctae Martae, 27 January 2015.

The truth of the Incarnation, made of humility and service, does not then admit of the 'spiritual worldliness' that is hidden behind appearances of religiosity and love for the Church, because that is a way of seeking one's own interests instead of Christ's (cf. Phil 2:21). It is a worldliness which is manifested in the Gnostic approach of those who consider faith to be purely subjective and live it by being imprisoned in their own thoughts and feelings; or in the Neopelagian approach, which is 'self-absorbed and promethean', of those who trust only in their own strength and feel they are superior to others, in the name of a 'supposed soundness of doctrine or discipline [which] leads instead to a narcissistic and authoritarian elitism' (*EG*, no. 94). This is the danger of an elite Church, characterized by a 'business mentality' but where 'the mark of Christ, incarnate, crucified and risen is not present' (*EG*, no. 95). Such attitudes are a reductionist representation of Christianity which marginalize the figure of Christ and diminish the scope of the Incarnation.

Worldliness, despite its appearance of good, is a 'tremendous corruption'. The Pope warns: 'We need to avoid it by making the Church constantly go out from herself, keeping her mission focused on Jesus Christ, and her commitment to the poor. God save us from a worldly Church with superficial spiritual and pastoral trappings! This stifling worldliness can only be healed by breathing in the pure air of the Holy Spirit who frees us from self-centredness cloaked in an outward religiosity bereft of God. Let us not allow ourselves to be robbed of the Gospel!' (*EG*, no. 97).

1.2 The fragility of the flesh

The salvific truth of the Incarnation is not shown through the outward signs of worldliness. Instead it is shown in the fragility of the body of Christ, offered as a gift for all humankind. In the fragility of the body of Christ we find the reason for salvation and sharing.[13]

The theme of the fragility of the body of Christ, dealt with predominantly in Eucharistic contexts, has strong Christological relevance. It is often found in Cardinal Bergoglio's preaching, especially in the Chrism celebrations on Holy Thursday and on the solemnity of *Corpus Domini*.

In the homily he gave for *Corpus Domini* 2003,[14] Bergoglio made reference to the biblical account of the Last Supper, and considered fragility 'not as a wound, as the weakness for which the strongest must take responsibility, but as an instrument of life. The loving fragility of the Eucharist.'[15] He describes it as 'Fragility that overflows with love and sharing.'[16]

Furthermore, the Lord who made himself a loaf of bread is broken in this fragility and given precisely through the sharing of this bread. This fragility contains the mystery of

---

13 Cf. JM BERGOGLIO, *Il tesoro della nostra creta* – Letter to catechists, August 2003, in JM BERGOGLIO – POPE FRANCIS, *È l'amore che apre gli occhi*, cit., 357.

14 JM BERGOGLIO, "He broke it and gave it to them" - *Homily, Corpus Domini*, 2003, in JM BERGOGLIO – POPE FRANCIS, *È l'amore che apre gli occhi*, cit., 314-317.

15 *Ibidem*, 314.

16 *Ivi*.

Christ and the secret of life of every individual and of the entire world.

At the Last Supper, Jesus handed himself over totally by 'breaking' himself. This Eucharistic gesture expresses the dynamic of Christ's Incarnation: he became incarnate, and on the cross he broke his own body, his life, to hand himself over completely as the bread of life and the gift of salvation for all humankind. One could say that the fragility of the Eucharistic bread, inasmuch as it is the bread of life, fully expresses the saving power of the fragility of the flesh he took on in his Incarnation. Bergoglio says: 'In the Eucharist, fragility is strength. The strength of love that makes itself weak so it can be received. The strength of love that is broken in order to nurture, give life and be shared in solidarity. Jesus who breaks bread with his hands! Jesus who gives himself in the Eucharist!'[17]

The message of hope and the gift of Jesus' salvation are present in the loving Eucharistic fragility of the Lord. In the light of this, Jesus' fragility becomes the strength of salvation and, in him, human fragility also acquires new meaning.[18] In fact, as Bergoglio explained in another homily for the celebration of *Corpus Domini*,[19] by his death on the cross he became the living bread, 'able to transform the multitude

---

17   *Ibidem*, 315.
18   Cf. *Ibidem*, 316-317.
19   JM BERGOGLIO, "*He began to speak to them about the kingdom of God*" - Homily, Corpus Domini, 2004, in JM BERGOGLIO – POPE FRANCIS, *È l'amore che apre gli occhi*, cit., 318-321.

into a community,'[20] to create community and nurture hope and solidarity.[21]

1.3 The 'limited' Incarnation

In his meditation, 'Faith of our fathers'[22] directed to the recovery and transmission of an integral and fruitful faith which is the foundation of religious identity and belonging to the Church, Bergoglio pauses to recall 'the Catholic image of God.' He says: 'He is not an absent figure. He is the father who accompanies growth, the daily bread that nurtures, the mercy that joins his children at times when the Enemy uses them. He is the father who, if it is the case, gives his children what they ask for but always caresses them. This means accepting that God expresses himself in *a limited way* and as a consequence it means accepting the limits of our pastoral expression (so far from the idea of the one who has the key to the world, who knows neither the expectation nor fatigue that lives by hysteria and illusion).'[23]

Then, referring to Paul VI's Apostolic Exhortation *Evangelii Nuntiandi* (*EN*), Bergoglio continues: 'Jesus, who

---

20 *Ibidem*, 320.

21 In another homily for *Corpus Domini*, Bergoglio stated that the account of the Last Supper contains an invitation to take two paths with Jesus and his disciples, in which the main player is the Eucharistic bread: the first is the path that leads to the Eucharist; the other is a path of hope with its origins in the Eucharist (cf. *"The Lord walks beside us" – Homily, Corpus Domini*, 2006, in JM BERGOGLIO – POPE FRANCIS, *È l'amore che apre gli occhi*, cit., 326.

22 Cf. JM BERGOGLIO – POPE FRANCIS, *Nel cuore di ogni padre. Alle radici della mia spiritualità*, cit., 127-135.

23 *Ibidem*, 131-132.

proclaims that God has expressed himself in a limited way in his Incarnation, wanted to share his life with human beings, and this is *redemption*. It was not only "the death and resurrection of Christ" that saved us, but Christ incarnate, who came into the world, fasted, preached, cared for people, died and was risen. The miracles, consolations, words of Jesus are salvific. In fact he wanted to teach us that syntheses are made, they do not arrive already complete; that to serve the holy, faithful, people of God means accompanying them by proclaiming salvation day after day, rather than losing ourselves by looking at unreachable peaks which we do not have the strength to reach.'[24]

This concept of 'limited incarnation' is particularly interesting. It is an image that does not intend to declare a limit to incarnation due to some lack or insufficiency, but instead seeks to present the notion of incarnation as a 'limited' expression of God and his power regarding human redemption. It means that incarnation is a work made to the 'measure' of the human being, a work made to the 'measure' of its purpose which is to share human life in order to carry out the divine plan for salvation of all humankind. This 'limited' work of God is the work of human redemption.

'Limited' incarnation is the expression of God's unlimited love. By taking on human flesh he redeems all humankind and also human relationships. In order to explain the link between the confession of faith and social commitment, Pope Francis states: 'To believe that the Son

---

24 *Ibidem*, 132

of God assumed our human flesh means that each human person has been taken up into the very heart of God. To believe that Jesus shed his blood for us removes any doubt about the boundless love which ennobles each human being. Our redemption has a social dimension because "God, in Christ, redeems not only the individual person, but also the social relations existing between men"' (*EG*, no. 178).[25]

1.4 Incarnation and the Christian mission

The Incarnation is the theological and pastoral foundation for the Church's mission which means going forth, going out of itself to go to its brothers and sisters. Jesus offered his flesh to save sinful flesh.[26] Pope Francis speaks about our brother or sister as 'the prolongation of the Incarnation for each one of us' (*EG*, no. 179), because what is done to a brother or sister in need is done to him.

The Lord's Incarnation is a truth which challenges faith and must have a real impact on the life of the Church and of every Christian.[27] In particular, it must characterize the

---

25 Here the Pope quotes THE PONTIFICAL COUNCIL FOR JUSTICE AND PEACE, *Compendium of the Social Doctrine of the Church*, no. 52).

26 "The Word made man remits the sins of the world through his passion; he takes on himself all suffering, all guilt. Jesus comes to sinful flesh and to save it, offers his own flesh (Col 2:14)." JM BERGOGLIO – POPE FRANCIS, *Aprite la mente al vostro cuore*, cit., 183).

27 "To enable us to know, accept and follow him, the Son of God took on our flesh ... Christian faith is faith in the Incarnation of the Word and his bodily resurrection; it is faith in a God who is so close to us that he entered our human history. Far from divorcing us from reality, our faith in the Son of God made man in

Church's work of evangelization, since 'The Incarnation of the Gospel in the life of the Church implies that the way in which Christ is preached and encountered will be different in different countries, different for people with different backgrounds ... a renewed preaching of the Gospel demands not merely that our lives be, and be seen to be, in conformity with the commitment to justice Christ demands of us, but also that the structures of theological reflection, catechesis, liturgy and pastoral ministry be adapted to needs perceived through a real experience of the situation.'[28]

The mission requires this commitment: a commitment that cannot be achieved by using some preconceived 'recipe' or theological 'touching up' but only by being available to learn from the people and the poor to whom we are rendering this service. It is from them that we need to learn the language and useful references for providing an adequate service which responds to the logic of the Incarnation. It is possible to help the poor only if we accept walking patiently and humbly with them, and only on condition that we agree to receive something from them.[29]

The readiness to walk with the poor demands an attitude of loyalty where the Incarnation of the Lord is concerned.

Jesus of Nazareth enables us to grasp reality's deepest meaning and to see how much God loves this world and is constantly guiding it towards himself. This leads us, as Christians, to live our lives in this world with ever greater commitment and intensity" (*LF, no. 18*).

28   32nd GENERAL CONGREGATION OF THE SOCIETY OF JESUS, *Decree* 4, 54.

29   Cf. JM BERGOGLIO – POPE FRANCIS, *Nel cuore di ogni padre. Alle radici della mia spiritualità*, cit., 257-258.

Bergoglio says that 'we will be able to learn to listen to the voice of the poor, who have one (though at times reduced by injustice to a whisper), instead of taking it upon ourselves to speak for them, in a language perhaps kilometres away from their desires and the aspirations of their heart.'[30] This is the basic and decisive criterion for evangelization, because it draws its inspiration from the Lord's Incarnation and finds its foundation in it.

Taking up the terms of Paul VI's Apostolic Exhortation *EN* once again, Pope Francis says: 'It is not about "disguising ourselves". It is about taking a deep approach as a model of evangelization, the *indivise et inconfuse* of the Lord. To be incarnate human beings "it is absolutely necessary for us to take into account a heritage of faith that the Church has the duty of preserving in its untouchable purity, and of presenting it to the people of our time, in a way that is as understandable and persuasive as possible."'[31]

The Pope applies a typically original and Christological formula to evangelization: *indivise et inconfuse* or 'without division and confusion'. This formula, in its Latin version, includes two of the four adverbs used in the Christological definition approved by the Ecumenical Council of Chalcedon in 451,[32] to explain the union of the divine and

---

30 *Ibidem*, 258.

31 *Ibidem*, 259. For the quote contained in the text, cf. PAUL VI, *EN*, no. 3.

32 Cf. H DENZINGER – A SCHÖNMETZER, *Enchiridion Symbolorum Definitionum et Declarationum de rebus fidei et morum*, Herder, Barcinone – Friburgi Brisgoviae – Romae 1976, nos 301-302.

human natures in the one person of Christ: this union took place in the Incarnation, 'without confusion', 'without change', 'without division', 'without separation'.[33] the four adverbs were used in the explanation of the mystery of the person of Christ to distance the definition from the errors of Eutyches and Nestorius: while the former considered the result of the union of natures to be a confused mixture, the latter was accused of maintaining the two natures to be separate and divided.

The Pope uses the formula to explain that evangelization needs to be carried out according the manner of the Incarnation, without confusion and division, without lessening and altering the integrity of the mystery of Christ, following the model of the *indivise et inconfuse* which is opposed to the *divise et confuse* which the Enemy practises,[34] wanting to divide and confuse.

This thought of Pope Francis' clarifies the fundamental terms of his pastoral activity and theological outlook. He says: 'The universality of evangelization … lies at the meeting point between the apostolic mission, adoption of the culture

---

33   The four adverbs used in the Greek text of the Chalcedonian definition are: *asynchýtos, atréptos, adiarétos and acorístos*; in the Latin version they are translated by *inconfuse, immutabiliter, indivise, inseparabiliter* respectively. Cf. H DENZINGER – A SCHÖNMETZER, *Enchiridion Symbolorum Definitionum et Declarationum de rebus fidei et morum*, cit., no. 302.

34   Cf. JM BERGOGLIO – POPE FRANCIS, *Nel cuore di ogni padre. Alle radici della mia spiritualità*, cit., 259. Cf. also A COZZI, *La verità di Dio e dell'uomo in Cristo. Il teologico e l'antropologico nella cristologia di J. BERGOGLIO*, in A COZZI – R REPOLE – G PIANA, *Papa Francesco. Quale teologia?*, Cittadella, Assisi 2016, 18-21.

of the people we are sent to, and our continued fidelity to the message received.'[35] The theological and pastoral paradigm which flows from the Incarnation has to be articulated on the basis of these three reasons: fidelity to the apostolic mission, taking up the culture of the people, and fidelity to the mission received.

2. *Anointing*

In strict rapport with the mystery of the Incarnation and of considerable Christological value, is Jesus' anointing. This is a topic Bergoglio has come back to often, especially in his homilies which are always an opportunity for him to explore the value of Jesus' mission and the intimate relationship it has with his identity.

In the homily he gave during the Chrism Mass in 2002,[36] taking his cue from the Gospel account of Jesus' visit to Nazareth and the address he gave in the synagogue (cf. Lk 4:21-30), Cardinal Bergoglio said: 'The Father anoints his Son, making him a man "for" others, to send him to proclaim the Good News, to heal and liberate. In the Son, everything comes from the Father, and at the same time, everything in him is "for" us.'[37] Jesus' anointing by the Father is the beginning of his mission on behalf of humankind and

---

35 JM BERGOGLIO – POPE FRANCIS, *Nel cuore di ogni padre. Alle radici della mia spiritualità*, cit., 260.

36 Cf. JM BERGOGLIO, *"He anointed him so he could recover, be free ..." – Homily, Chrism Mass, 2002*, in JM BERGOGLIO – POPE FRANCIS, *È l'amore che apre gli occhi,* cit., 250-254.

37 *Ibidem*, 250.

the act that makes him a man 'totally for others'. In Jesus, everything is from the Father, but through the anointing that 'everything from the Father' becomes 'everything for human beings'.

Bergoglio explains that anointing is not about purely external gestures of the person but concerns the person's inner disposition. The anointing not only determines the power of Jesus' actions and gestures but permeates the depths of his person and allows him to live in communion with the Father. This makes Christ a gift of salvation for others 'today'.[38] The encounter with Christ is a *kairós* for human beings, meaning it becomes a propitious opportunity for salvation for everyone. Bergoglio says: 'His strength ... is not measured on the basis of the number of miracles the Anointed of the Lord works, nor how far away he carries out his mission, not even by the gravity of his suffering: the depth of the anointing, which penetrates his very bones, and the efficacy through which everything in him is salvation for those who approach him, sink their roots into the intimate union and total identification with the Father who sent him

---

38 Bergoglio thus explains the fulfilment today of salvation in encountering Jesus: "The mission is achieved 'today' because the Lord does not limit himself to giving bread: he makes himself bread. The liberation he gives to the oppressed takes place 'today', insofar as the Lord does not limit himself to forgiving, 'cleaning the stains' off other's clothing: He himself becomes sin, soiled, covered in wounds. And by doing this he entrusts himself into the hands of the Father who accepts him. The Good News, finally, is realized 'today' because the Lord does not limit himself to announcing that he will take measures – he himself becomes the measure that helps us to see the light through his every word' (*Ibidem*, 252).

among us.'[39] The anointing forms and prepares the individual for the work of salvation.[40]

Because of the anointing he received from the Father, Christ does not simply carry out a task of healing, and liberation from some illness or oppression, but is led to give himself totally. To understand this notion even better, it could be useful to keep in mind a passage from another homily at a Chrism Mass,[41] where Bergoglio says: 'The Lord's action does not consist in merely carrying out a task ... but in a mission that, for him, implies the total gift of himself and, for the beneficiaries of such a gift, unhesitating acceptance of it. It is precisely here where the true meaning of anointing lies – it is a gift. Only someone who has received it can then anoint others in turn and only someone who strips himself of

---

39 *Ivi.*

40 Due to priestly anointing, the priestly ministry also demands the same dynamic of gift. In fact, addressing his priests directly, Bergoglio says: "We too, my dear brother priests, have been anointed so we can anoint in turn, and thus enter into total communion with Jesus and the Father. So, just as in baptism, the priestly anointing acts from within toward the outside. In spite of appearances, the priesthood is not a grace that comes from outside and does not succeed in penetrating the heart of the sinner. On the contrary, we are priests deep within, in the sacred and mysterious space of our soul, where we become sons through baptism and where we acknowledge the Trinity. The moral effort we have to carry out consists in anointing our daily gestures toward our neighbour, such that our whole life is truly transformed, thanks to our commitment, into what it has already become by virtue of the grace we have received" (*Ibidem, 252-253*).

41 *Cf.* JM BERGOGLIO, *"Jesus' homily was very short ..."* – Homily, Chrism Mass, 2006, in *JM BERGOGLIO – POPE FRANCIS, È l'amore che apre gli occhi, cit., 266-271.*

everything can be consecrated. Jesus, the beloved Son, is the Anointed One *par excellence* insofar as he receives everything from the Father. He possesses nothing and does nothing for himself: in him, everything is anointing and fulfilment of the mission. And as he accepted everything in himself, he gives his life through the sacrifice of the cross.'[42] By virtue of his anointing, in his relationship with the Father, Jesus becomes the gift of salvation for all humankind.

3. The cross

The culminating moment of Jesus' mission and of the total gift he made of himself is the cross. In that event, the fullness of the mystery of the Incarnation and of the whole mystery of Christ is realized and manifested, with all its implications for Christian identity and mission. Up till now, Pope Francis has dealt with these aspects, broadly and in some depth, in his essentially spiritual interventions, especially in preaching. Here the perspective and content seem to be essentially inspired by the spirituality of St Ignatius of Loyola, founder of the Society of Jesus, and above all from the topics and tone of the *Spiritual Exercises* (*SE*).

3.1 Passion in the flesh

In his meditation on St Ignatius of Loyola's *Spiritual Exercises*, the Jesuit Bergoglio is contemplating the passion in Jesus' flesh: 'This man Jesus, who is God, but who suffers

---

42 *Ibidem*, 268-269.

as a man, in his own body, in his own psyche.'[43] Jesus really faced up to his passion and death with dignity and freedom, accepting the Father's handing him over.[44] 'His freedom is such that he accepts both the Father's purpose (that he be handed over), and the instrument employed (being killed in a certain way by real individuals). What shines out here is the dignity of Christ who exclaims: "Worthy is the Lamb" (Rev 5:12). It is the dignity of someone who abandons himself in obedience to the will of the Father, and who accepts this will and also the way in which it is to happen and, at the same time. He does all this with the greatest of freedom.'[45]

In the full acceptance of the Father's will, Jesus offers himself, humiliating himself to the point of total self-spoliation. We are talking about an 'annihilation' which has gone as far as death on the cross. While being considered a prophet (cf. Mt 21:11; Lk 7:16; Jn 4:19; 9:17), it is not death by stoning (cf. Mt 23:37; Lk 13:33) as the Jewish law prescribed for false prophets and blasphemers. He died as a political conspirator and someone accursed, someone 'hung up on a tree' outside the walls of Jerusalem (cf. Dt 21:22).[46]

---

43 JM BERGOGLIO – POPE FRANCIS, *Aprite la mente al vostro cuore* cit., 235.

44 On the matter of Jesus' acceptance of death and the completeness of his self-dispossession, some ideas are drawn from H COUSIN, *Il profeta assassinato: storia dei testi della Passione*, Borla, Rome 1976.

45 JM BERGOGLIO – POPE FRANCIS, *Aprite la mente al vostro cuore* cit., 238.

46 Cf. *Ibidem*, 239-241.

This death, while the work of human beings, happened to fulfil God's plan[47] and became the reason for our salvation. With a reference to St Maximus the Confessor, Bergoglio explains the redemption in terms of the patristic theory of the trap set for the devil: in humiliation and despoliation, Jesus becomes 'bait' for Satan. By believing he is a man like all others, he is poisoned by the divinity.[48] God manifests his saving power through his human impotence.

3.2 The failure of the flesh

The passion and death represent Jesus' failure.[49] Betrayed by Judas and left alone by his other disciples, Jesus dies as a failed human being. It is an historic failure which he really experiences in the 'flesh'.[50] This is a failure that cannot be

---

47   "Jesus' death is the work of men, but the plan is divine; the work of men is, in turn, the 'work' of God: 'The Son of Man is to be betrayed into human hands, and they will kill him, and three days after being killed, he will rise again' (Mk 9:31). 'Betrayed into human hands' and 'kill' have technical meanings in the Scriptures. 'Killing' refers to the assassination of the just man and points to men as the authors of death. The verb 'betray' or 'hand over' instead, indicates that God is the author of this handing over: 'He who did not withhold his own Son, but gave him up for all of us' (Rom 8:32)" (*Ibidem*, 237).

48   "Thus he believes he has overcome and eaten the flesh … that is not flesh for him but bait, a hook within which is the poison the ultimately kills him: the divinity." Bergoglio is quoting MAXIMUS THE CONFESSOR, *Centurie* I, 8-13 (PG 90, 1182-1186). Cf. JM BERGOGLIO – POPE FRANCIS, *Aprite la mente al vostro cuore*, cit., 239.

49   On the theme of Jesus' failure, Bergoglio has taken up some ideas from the third chapter of the work by J NAVONE, *Teologia del fallimento*, Pontifical Gregorian University, Rome, 1988.

50   Cf. JM BERGOGLIO – POPE FRANCIS, *Aprite la mente al*

disguised, not even with the 'common sense' interpretations common to ecclesiastical elites. To ignore the failure of the cross would mean denying the reality of Jesus' flesh and falling into neo-docetism. 'They are neo-docetists and, ultimately, they are not very convinced that Jesus, the Christ, is alive in his body, is risen. At most they accept a resurrection rather closer to the Bultmannian notion, or a spiritualist resurrection, simply because they have denied Christ's flesh by not accepting its failure.'[51]

Jesus' passion and death were no pretence nor were they a myth. As the high priest of future goods,[52] he offered his flesh and blood as a sacrifice for the sins of all humankind through his total annihilation and acceptance of his own failure,[53] Bergoglio emphasizes that: 'The priesthood of Christ is exercised in three stages: in the sacrifice on the cross (and in this sense it was "once and for all"); currently (as intercessor with the Father, Heb 7:25); and at the end of time ("not to deal with sin" Heb 9:28). when Christ will hand all of creation over to the Father.'[54]

Only by accepting the failure of the cross in the flesh is it possible to have access to the Father. There is a need for us to share with our own flesh in the passion of Christ's flesh

vostro cuore, cit., 242.245.

51 Cf. *Ibidem*, 244.

52 Cf. *Ibidem*, 246-248.

53 Bergoglio develops his reflection on the Letter to Hebrews with reference especially to the following passages: Heb 2:17-18; 7:26-28; 9:11-14; 10:12.

54 JM BERGOGLIO – POPE FRANCIS, *Aprite la mente al vostro cuore,* cit., 247.

in order to also share in his resurrection and glorification: 'In the mysteries of the resurrection, Jesus, who has already become Lord, shows himself in his body, lets his wounds, his flesh be touched (Jn 20:20, 27; Lk 24:39, 42). That body, those wounds, that flesh are intercession. It goes further: There is no other access to the Father other than this. The Father sees the flesh of his Son and makes it gain access to salvation … We find the Father in Jesus' wounds. He is alive, then, in his glorious flesh and is alive in us.'[55] Faced with the powerlessness of human means, God really intervenes with the power of resurrection and, through Christ's flesh, offers access to salvation: 'The resurrection of Jesus Christ is the not end of a film: it is God's intervention given the total impossibility of human hope; the intervention which proclaims as "Lord" the one who accepted the way of failure so that the power of the Father would be manifested and glorified.'[56]

3.3 Christian life as 'struggle'

Following the path laid out by St Ignatius Loyola's *SE*,[57] a true and proper path of discernment[58] on decisions

---

55 *Ivi*, 247.
56 *Ibidem*, 242-243.
57 Cf. JM Bergoglio – Pope Francis, *Il desiderio allarga il cuore. Esercizi spirituali con il Papa*, EMI, Bologna 2014; S Rendina, *L'itinerario degli Esercizi spirituali di sant'Ignazion di Loyola. Commento introduttivo alle quattro settimane*, AdP, Rome 1999, 2004.
58 On discernment, cf. F Rossi De Gasperis – I De La Potterie, *Il discernmineto spirituale del cristiano, oggi*, FIES, Rome 1988; M Ruz Jurado, *Il discernimento spirituale*, Paoline,

to be taken and choices to be made,[59] Bergoglio explains in the meditation for the second week, known as 'The Two Standards',[60] that it deals with the choice between two roads: the one proposed by Christ, made up of poverty, insults and humility, and that of the Devil which offers wealth, vainglory and pride.

What immediately emerges here is the 'warlike' nature of Christian discipleship, and the 'combative' dimension of the faith typical of Ignatian spirituality: in order to follow Christ we need to fight his battle, the battle he fought on the cross and which he won, but which still goes on in history and within each human being. Faith is 'combative', not in the sense of a combativeness aimed at conflict, but of dedication to the purpose of the Spirit.[61]

In the dimension of life which the Greeks call '*agon*' or struggle, discernment takes on crucial importance as a

---

Cinisello Balsamo (MI) 1997; S FAUSTI, *Occasione o tentazione? Arte di discernere e decidere*, Àncora, Milan 1997; P SCHIAVONE, *Il discernimento. Teoria e prassi,* Paoline, Milan 2009, 2011.

59 The complete title of the booklet with the *Spiritual Exercises* is especially expressive: "Spiritual Exercises which have as their purpose the conquest of self and the regulation of one's life in such a way that no decision is made under the influence of any inordinate attachment" (*SE* no. 21).

60 *SE*, no. 136. Cf. JM BERGOGLIO – POPE FRANCIS, *Nel cuore di ogni padre. Alle radici della mia spiritualità*, cit., 162-169.

61 "Our faith is revolutionary, and a foundation in itself. It is *a combative faith*, but not a combative faith aimed at conflict as such; rather is it dedicated to a purpose which the Spirit's guidance has allowed us discern in order to serve the Church better, and, on the other hand, to receive the potential for being liberated not from ideologies, but from contact with the holy: it is hierophantic" (*Ibidem*, 128).

decisive means in the struggle to follow the Lord closely, meaning to follow him along the same road he took, and follow him in the same lifestyle. Discernment is necessary in order not to be fooled 'by the evil spirit' and to be able to follow 'the good spirit.'[62]

The criterion for Ignatian discernment, based on the warning from the Apostle John, focuses on recognizing the mystery of Christ: 'By this you know the Spirit of God: every spirit that confesses that Jesus Christ has come in the flesh is from God, and every spirit that does not confess Jesus is not from God' (1 Jn 4:2-3).

The good spirit leads us to believe in the Incarnation and to proclaim Jesus Christ, the Word of God made flesh; the evil spirit, with his divisive approach, rejects the Incarnation and humiliation of the Word, and leads to denying unity and urges us to distance ourselves from Christ and his Church: 'It is precisely of the spirit of God to confess that the Word of God became flesh, *indivise et inconfuse*. It strikes us that any deviation which has taken place in the Church throughout

---

62   There does not seem to be complete agreement among commentators on the *SE* on the meaning of the term 'spirit': according to some authors it could indicate the 'movements' of affectivity which move us to act; according to others it would indicate the agent which causes these movements, that is, the *good spirit* that move us toward the good and which can be attributed to the Holy Spirit, or the *evil spirit* or devil who moves us toward what is bad. Cf. S RENDINA, "Spiritual motions" and "discernment" in the Spiritual Exercises, in *'"Mozioni spirituali" e "discernimento" negli Esercizi spirituali'* in Proceedings of the National Convention, autumn 1998. Reports, documents, summary of group work, (Appunti di Spiritualità, 50), Centro Ignaziano di Spiritualità (C.I.S.), Naples 2000, 21-22.

history has had a strong effect on the Body of the Lord or on the Eucharist, or on the poor (who are the suffering body of Christ) or on the body of the Church, especially regarding union with its head. We make our discernment beginning with faith in the Word of God incarnate, born of the Virgin Mary by the work of the Holy Spirit, who suffered and died under Pontius Pilate and rose on the third day. We make our discernment beginning from faith in Christ, true God and true man, whose human nature is united *indivise et inconfuse* with his divinity.'[63]

Instead, the evil spirit, through confusion and division (*divise et confuse*) feeds this lie and extends it to the cross, where he is ultimately vanquished.[64] The cross is the place in which the good spirit shows himself totally, because the truth of the Incarnation of the Son of God becomes obvious there. When the cross manifests itself through the power of the resurrection, then we see how false the lie is, and it loses all its force.

This dimension, which marked Jesus' mission, characterizes the apostolic life too, and Christian existence because life is a 'struggle'. It is a struggle that is won by putting on the 'armour of God' which is the cross.[65] In the

63 JM Bergoglio – Pope Francis, *Nel cuore di ogni padre. Alle radici della mia spiritualità*, cit., 163.

64 *Ibidem*, 167.

65 "Christian life is like an army, it involves struggle, but just the same 'our struggle is not against enemies of blood and flesh, but against the rulers, against the authorities, against the cosmic powers of this present darkness, against the spiritual forces of evil in the heavenly places' (Eph 6:12). In order to win this battle, we do not need weapons made especially for it: we need the 'armour of

Christian life, then, we need to struggle and need to learn to struggle 'in a divine way'. Bergoglio says: 'Understanding the belligerent dimension of the apostolic life implies recognizing that in our heart, if we want to serve God, there has to be a struggle, understood as the search for the cross inasmuch as it is the only theological place of victory; a struggle which understands the capacity to condemn and the generosity of dedicating oneself to the most difficult and laborious of works. Proceeding along this road will bring us, like the Lord, to Jerusalem.'[66] Life's struggle is considered within the Christological perspective of conformation to Christ: living as Christ lived in order to arrive in Jerusalem as he did.

The cross profoundly marks the existence and mission of the Christian in his or her belonging to the Church, because it is the place where the Church is born. The Church was born at the hour of the Lord's death. So, the origin of the Church and foundation of Christian life are found in the cross. Without the cross there is no Christian life.[67]

God' (*ibidem*) in order to 'withstand ... and having done everything, to stand firm' (6:13); and the armour of God is the cross. It is there that the Evil One is beaten once and for all. When we take up the cross as salvation then we see within that 'the battle is not yours but God's' (2 Chron 20:15) and that it is He who is fighting for us" (*Ibidem* 194).

66   JM BERGOGLIO – POPE FRANCIS, *Aprite la mente al vostro cuore*, cit., 64.

67   Cf. A COZZI, *La verità di Dio e dell'uomo in Cristo. Il teologico e l'antropologico nella cristologia di J. Bergoglio*, cit., 13-67, 36-40.

3.4 The 'final battle'

The Ignatian perspective, called 'the belligerent meaning of life'[68] shows up another dimension of the cross which is fundamental for the mission of Jesus Christ and Christian existence.

The cross is the place where God fought the war for the salvation of humankind.: 'The cross is the "final battle" of Jesus: that is where his ultimate victory lies.'[69] The cross is the place where he pronounced his definitive 'Yes' of obedience which ransomed us from our original disobedience; it is the place where the "ancient serpent" was vanquished, the one who gave origin to rebellion and sin; it is the place where Christians become sons and daughters in the Son, with Mary as their Mother, who was right there at the foot of the cross.[70]

There is an echo of this in the Apostolic Exhortation *EG*: 'Christian triumph is always a cross, yet a cross which is at the same time a victorious banner borne with aggressive tenderness against the assaults of evil' (*EG*, no. 85).[71]

The Christian way of living expects that we follow Jesus's road, a road that inevitably leads to the cross. Jesus put it clearly himself: 'Whoever loves father or mother more than me is not worthy of me; and whoever loves son or daughter

---

68 JM Bergoglio – Pope Francis, *Aprite la mente al vostro cuore*, cit., 63-70.

69 *Ibidem*, 63.

70 *Ivi*.

71 Also: "The Christian triumph is always a cross, but a cross that is a victorious standard" (M Bergoglio – Pope Francis, *Nel cuore di ogni padre. Alle radici della mia spiritualità*, cit., 129).

more than me is not worthy of me; and whoever does not take up the cross and follow me is not worthy of me. Those who find their life will lose it, and those who lose their life for my sake will find it' (Mt 10:37-39).

In genuine Christian living there is always the certainty of the cross which shows up in many different ways through difficulties, obstacles, and persecutions. They are situations that Jesus had announced to his disciples and for which he had encouraged them to suffer (cf. Lk 6:22; Ml 8:35; 13:8-13; Mt 10:39), by imitating his passion (cf. Mt 10:22-23; Mk 10:38). Bergoglio suggests re-reading Stephen's martyrdom (Acts 6:8–7:60) as a paradigm of Christian experience. He explains: 'Stephen did not only die for Christ but dies like him, with him, and this sharing in the very mystery of the passion of Jesus Christ is the basis of the faith of the martyr: dying as a persecuted individual, expressing with his life that death is not the last word in Jesus' life.'[72]

When the Christian does not consider persecutions to be human punishments (cf. Mt 23:29-36); Acts 7:51-52) or eschatological judgement on works (cf. 1 Thess 2:15 ff; Mt 5:10-12), but faces them as did Stephen, then that person's life is a suffering and dying 'for the Son of Man'. This way of living likens the human being to Christ and makes him or her capable of gratitude, Eucharistic gratitude. In fact, the celebration of the Eucharist is about giving thanks for conformation to the death of the Lord, in our belonging to the Church.[73]

---

[72] JM Bergoglio – Pope Francis, *Aprite la mente al vostro cuore*, cit., 65-67.
[73] *Ibidem*, 65-67.

3.5 The hour of glory

The cross is not only the hour of the passion and death of the Lord and the image of Christian life as struggle, but is also the hour of glory. 'The patient, annihilated Christ is the glory of God. The glorious Christ risen in the flesh and spirit, is the glory of God.'[74]

Jesus' glory begins with his death on the cross. In this regard, Bergoglio recalls various New Testament texts, beginning with a passage from Luke's Gospel: 'Was it not necessary that the Messiah should suffer these things and then enter into his glory?' (Lk 24:26).[75] For Jesus, the cross is the way to glory. But it is not just so for him. It is the same for every Christian who gives his life for Jesus' cause.

It is significant that he explicitly quotes three verses from John's Gospel, not continuous ones, but setting them out in such a way that it is clear that what is true for Jesus also produces its effects in the Christian who loses his or her life in conformity with him. With regard to Christ he says: 'Jesus answered them, "The hour has come for the Son of Man to be glorified ... unless a grain of wheat falls into the earth and dies, it remains just a single grain; but if it dies, it bears much fruit' (Jn 12:23-24); he then quotes the following verse referring to all Christians: 'Those who love their life lose it, and those who hate their life in this world will keep it for eternal life' (Jn 12:25). In this way the Pope is pointing to the strict relationship between the glory that

---

74   *Ibidem*, 249.
75   Cf. *Ibidem*, 67.

comes from the cross of Christ and the loss of life of those who in their own lives follow the Lord as far as the cross.[76]

This is true, but it is difficult to understand. John's Gospel notes that the disciples too did not understand that the cross was the glory of Jesus; they understood this later: 'when Jesus was glorified, then they remembered that these things had been written of him and had been done to him' (Jn 12:16).

The glory of the cross, instead, was immediately recognized and exalted by St Paul. For him the cross of Christ became a reason for boasting, because in his conformation to Christ on the cross he recognized the reason for salvation and joy: 'May I never boast of anything except the cross of our Lord Jesus Christ, by which the world has been crucified to me, and I to the world' (Gal 6:14).[77] This means making the cross the instrument for combating human presumption and vainglory and thus coming to the point of receiving the glory of God. Bergoglio states: 'Adherence to the cross as a radically central element is, in the final instance, what inspires the criterion of truth of faithful discipleship of our Master.'[78]

Adherence to the cross is the decisive criterion which manifests truth and fidelity in our following of Christ. The cross becomes the 'centre of gravity' of Christian life.[79] It is not possible to ignore or forget it. Indeed, it is essential

76 *Ivi.*
77 Cf. *Ivi.*
78 *Ibidem*, 68.
79 *Ivi.*

to have 'a keen and continuous memory of the cross.'[80] The memory of the Lord's cross allows us to always find consolation and peace in our trials. In particular, it allows us to abandon ourselves into God's hands with confidence, even in suffering, in agony, as did Jesus.

Here it could be useful to recall the recommendation St Peter addressed to the Christians: 'Beloved, do not be surprised at the fiery ordeal that is taking place among you to test you, as though something strange were happening to you. But rejoice insofar as you are sharing Christ's' sufferings, so that you may also be glad and shout for joy when his glory is revealed. If you are reviled for the name of Christ, you are blessed, because the spirit of glory, which is the Spirit of God, is resting on you. But let none of you suffer as a murderer, a thief, a criminal, or even as a mischief maker. Yet if any of you suffers as a Christian, do not consider it a disgrace, but glorify God because you bear this name ... Therefore, let those suffering in accordance with God's will entrust themselves to a faithful Creator, while continuing to do good.' (1 Pt 4:12-19).

In the light of the Apostle's words, we understand even better that Christian life is marked by the cross and that it cannot be separated from it. There are no alternative routes or shortcuts for the Christian. There is only the road that Jesus took, the road that passes through the experience of abandonment into the Father's hands, with the preparedness to feel this abandonment by the Father. To this reflection

---

80 *Ivi.*

the Pope adds: 'The sense of abandonment into the Father's hands and the sense of being abandoned by the Father which every cross brings with it, shows the eschatological nature of this "milestone" in our Christian life. On the cross one needs to lose everything in order to conquer everything.'[81] As the Gospel says, it is about selling everything in order to buy the precious stone or the field where the treasure is hidden. Without forgetting that Jesus said: 'For those who want to save their life will lose it, and those who lose their life for my sake will find it' (Mt 16:25; Mk 8:34 ff; Lk 17:33). Only by losing everything can one have new life.[82]

To conclude, Pope Francis' words become even more effective: 'The cross marks the belligerent meaning of our existence. One cannot negotiate, cannot dialogue with the cross: we either embrace it or reject it. If we decide to reject it, our life will remain in our hands, trapped within our narrow horizons. If we choose to embrace it, we lose our life, place it in God's hands, in his time, and it will be given back to us only in another way.'[83]

---

81 *Ibidem*, 69.
82 Cf. *Ibidem*, 70.
83 *Ivi*

Chapter 3
THE KERYGMA OF LIFE

The *kerygma* is the principal and essential announcement of the Christian faith aimed at eliciting conversion and salvation in the recognition that Jesus Christ who died and rose, is the Lord. Pope Francis states that this is the first proclamation of the Father's infinite mercy, communicated through the death and resurrection of Jesus Christ, and that it should be 'the centre of all evangelizing activity and all efforts at Church renewal' (*Evangelii Gaudium*, no. 164, *EG*).

The *kerygma* however, is not simply a truth we must ascribe to but a content that the Church and each Christian must accept and pass on. Furthermore, it is a content that cannot be accepted and passed on in words alone, but through life, in all of its material and spiritual aspects, regularly in different situations and gradually across the range of historical circumstances, both personal and ecclesial, through words, choices and concrete gestures, in the process of conformation to Christ.

The *kerygma*, then, is the formula that expresses the essential core of faith, but is also the paradigm for conforming Christian life to the mystery of Christ. In this sense, the title of this chapter, 'the *kerygma* of life' refers both to the dimension of life and Easter hope which is the source of life, constitutive of this life, and to the program it offers Christian life.

After having considered the contents in earlier chapters, our attention now turns to the experiential dynamic of Christological faith in an effort to grasp some of its basic motivations, especially the primacy of Christ in the personal encounter with him, the option for the poor and conformation to his mystery.

In Pope Francis' perspective, in fact, for a knowledge of Christ and his mystery of love and salvation, we cannot ignore the Christian life experience of sharing in the Church's mission through the service and gift of oneself.

1. *The primacy of Christ*

The Apostolic Exhortation *EG* begins thus: 'The joy of the gospel fills the hearts and lives of all who encounter Jesus' because it is by staying with him that 'joy is constantly born anew' (*EG*, no. 1). From this comes the immediate invitation addressed to every Christian to renew his or her personal encounter with Jesus Christ 'or at least an openness to letting him encounter them; I ask all of you to do this unfailingly each day' (*EG*, No. 3). The Pope thus immediately highlights the Christological foundation for joy and underlines in particular the importance of Christian experience. The focus is on the encounter with Christ, 'personal encounter with Christ'. Furthermore, the Pope adds: 'No one should think that this invitation is not meant for him or her, since "no one is excluded from the joy brought by the Lord".[1] The Lord does not disappoint those who take this risk; whenever

---

1 A quote from Paul VI, *Gaudete in Domino*, Apostolic Exhortation, 9 May 1975, no. 22, in *AAS* 67 (1975), 289-322, 297.

we take a step towards Jesus, we come to realize that he is already there, waiting for us with open arms' (*EG*, no. 3).

With these words the Pope recalls two fundamental motivations for Christian experience. They are not new, since he has already insisted on them previously: the primacy of God and the need for personal encounter with Christ.

1.1 The almond blossom

Christian experience begins through the action of divine grace,[2] because God always precedes the human being with his mercy and love. St John says this effectively: 'In this is love, not that we loved God but that he loved us' (I Jn 4:10). Even though the human being asks questions and seeks God in various ways, in real terms it is God who first encourages this search and waits for it. It is he who takes the initiative because his love always precedes any love on the part of the human being.

Pope Francis loves to represent the primacy of God in the history of his people and in the life of humankind with a prophetic image, the almond blossom,[3] the tree that flowers

---

2 In no. 112 of the Apostolic Exhortation *EG,* Pope Francis states the principle of the primacy of grace also where the evangelizing activity of the Church is concerned, quoting a reflection of Pope Benedict XVI's: "It is important always to know that the first word, the true initiative, the true activity comes from God and only by inserting ourselves into the divine initiative, only begging for this divine initiative, shall we too be able to become – with him and in him – evangelizers" (*Meditation during the first General Congregation of the 13th Ordinary General Aassembly of the Synod of Bishops*, 8 October 21012, in AAS 104 [2012], 895-900, 897.

3 Cf. Jer 1:11-12. Cf. POPE FRANCIS, *La mia porta è sempre*

before others and is first to announce the coming of spring. The image is used to say that God, as the 'almond blossom', anticipates any human initiative.

God has always taken the initiative in the history of salvation, and in many different ways, and has taken the first step to encounter his people, listening to their cry, succouring them and freeing them from every kind of slavery and oppression. This anticipatory way of acting reached its culmination in the mystery of the Incarnation, given that God's initiative is fully manifested in Christ. In the Encyclical *Lumen Fidei* (*LF*) the Pope explains that salvation begins with the opening 'to something prior to ourselves, to a primordial gift that affirms life and sustains it in being. Only by being open to and acknowledging this gift can we be transformed, experience salvation and bear good fruit (*LF*, no. 19).[4] Then he also adds: 'Faith's new way of seeing things is centred on Christ. Faith in Christ brings salvation because in him our lives become radically open to a love that precedes us, a love that transforms us from within, acting in us and through us' (*LF*, no. 20).

On the Solemnity of the Epiphany in 2014, commenting on the sign of the star which appeared to the Magi to point to the birth of Christ, the Pope explained that if they had

---

aperta. Una conversazione con Antonio Spadaro, Rizzoli, Milan 2013, 98. This work is available in English as *My Door Is Always Open: A Conversation on Faith, Hope and the Church in a Time of Change*, Bloomsbury 2014.

4 In this context, the Pope also says: 'Salvation by faith means recognizing the primacy of God's gift. As Saint Paul puts it: "By grace you have been saved through faith, and this is not your own doing; it is the gift of God" (Eph 2:8).

not seen the star, they would not have left on their journey. The star which appeared to the Magi, then, was a sign of the divine initiative for the salvation of humankind: 'And God goes ever before, he is always the first to seek us, he takes the first step. God goes ever before us. His grace precedes us and this grace appeared in Jesus. He is the Epiphany. He, Jesus Christ, is the manifestation of God's love. He is with us.'[5] Jesus Christ, who is God and man, shows God's initiative and precedence where human beings are concerned.

The primacy of the Lord's initiative is found in the Apostolic Exhortation *EG*, where Pope Francis expresses the need for a missionary transformation of the Church and the describes the Church 'going forth' as a community of disciples able to 'take the initiative' and 'involve themselves' in human history (cf. *EG*, no. 24). The Pope expresses this need with a neologism, *primerear* (take the first step), which he presents in a clearly Christological sense.[6] In fact he explains that it is an urgency that comes from the experience that the Lord is the one who takes the initiative and always 'gets involved and involves his own.' The Pope writes: 'An

---

5   Pope Francis, *Angelus*, Epiphany of the Lord, 6 January 2014. Cf. also: *Homily*, Mass at Domus Sanctae Marthae, 8 January 2015; cf. also *Address to the Communion and Liberation Movement*, St Peter's Square, 7 March 2015. The same image of the almond blossom was used by Bergoglio on three earlier occasions, for example, during the homily at the Easter Vigil in the Metropolitan Cathedral at Buenos Aires on 22 April 200) (Cf. JM Bergoglio – Pope Francis, *Omelie Pasquali*, cit., 6; cf. also JM Bergoglio, *"L'angelo rassicura le donne: 'Non abbiate paura!'*, in JM Bergoglio – Pope Francis, *È l'amore che apre gli occhi,* cit., 278.

6   On the use of *primerear*, cf. also the *Address to the Communion and Liberation Movement*, St Peter's Square, 7 March 2015.

evangelizing community knows that the Lord has taken the initiative, he has loved us first (cf. 1 Jn 4:19), and therefore we can move forward, boldly take the initiative, go out to others, seek those who have fallen away, stand at the crossroads and welcome the outcast. Such a community has an endless desire to show mercy, the fruit of its own experience of the power of the Father's infinite mercy' (*EG*, no. 24).[7]

The Christological connotation clearly emerges when the Pope illustrates the real ways in which the Church must 'get involved' with others: it must do so following Jesus' example, who gets on his knees to wash the feet of his disciples (Jn 13:17). The Pope writes thus: 'An evangelizing community gets involved by word and deed in people's daily lives; it bridges distances, it is willing to abase itself if necessary, and it embraces human life, touching the suffering flesh of Christ in others' (*EG*, no. 24). Thus it is that the evangelizers take on 'the smell of the sheep' and succeed in being listened to by the sheep.

The Church must accompany humanity with Christ's attentive and anticipatory approach, acting such that in every concrete situation the Word is embodied and bears the fruit of new life. Pope Francis points out the way: 'The disciple is ready to put his or her whole life on the line, even to accepting martyrdom, in bearing witness to Jesus Christ, yet the goal is not to make enemies but to see God's word accepted and its capacity for liberation and renewal revealed' (*EG*, no. 24).

7   On the primacy of God and grace in evangelization, cf. also *EG*, nos 12 and 112.

The citing of texts from Paul VI's Encyclical *Ecclesiam Suam*[8] and the Decree on Ecumenism *Unitatis Redintegratio*[9] from Vatican Council II (cf. *EG*, no. 26) also echoes this Christological anchorage. Indeed, as an introduction to the Council's text the Pope writes: 'The Second Vatican Council presented ecclesial conversion as openness to a constant self-renewal born of fidelity to Jesus Christ' (*EG*, no. 26).

1.2 The personal encounter with Christ

The fundamental experience of Christian life, true discipleship and any commitment to evangelization is the personal encounter with the Lord and remaining close to him.[10] This encounter is possible only to the extent of

---

8 Paul VI, *Ecclesiam Suam*, Encyclical, 6 August 1964, nos 10-12: "The Church must look with penetrating eyes within herself, ponder the mystery of her own being... This vivid and lively self-awareness inevitably leads to a comparison between the ideal image of the Church as Christ envisaged her and loved her as his holy and spotless bride (cf. Eph 5:27), and the actual image which the Church presents to the world today... This is the source of the Church's heroic and impatient struggle for renewal: the struggle to correct those flaws introduced by her members which her own self-examination, mirroring her exemplar, Christ, points out to her and condemns"

9 "Every renewal of the Church essentially consists in an increase of fidelity to her own calling... Christ summons the Church as she goes her pilgrim way... to that continual reformation of which she always has need, in so far as she is a human institution here on earth" (*UR*, no. 6).

10 The Pope writes that 'it is not the same thing to have known Jesus as not to have known him, not the same thing to walk with him as to walk blindly, not the same thing to hear his word as not to know it, and not the same thing to contemplate him, to worship him, to find our peace in him, as not to. It is not the same

openness to the action of divine grace,[11] and is the essence of Christian identity and the foundation for every vocation.[12] Only by beginning with the encounter with God, in fact, is it possible to be genuine witnesses of Christ and exercise 'the diaconate of tenderness', also in the face of experience of sadness and suffering.[13]

Picking up the contents of the Apostolic Letter *Novo Millennio Ineunte* (NMI), by John Paul II at the end of

---

thing to try to build the world with his Gospel as to try to do so by our own lights. We know well that with Jesus life becomes richer and that with him it is easier to find meaning in everything. This is why we evangelize. A true missionary, who never ceases to be a disciple, knows that Jesus walks with him, speaks to him, breathes with him, works with him. He senses Jesus alive with him in the midst of the missionary enterprise' (*EG* no. 266). Then Francis adds: 'In union with Jesus, we seek what he seeks and we love what he loves' (*EG* no. 267).

11 The Pope reminds the clergy that the encounter with Christ does not depend on personal abilities, the spectacular nature of ecclesial initiatives or the cleverness of pastoral plans: "It is not in soul-searching or constant introspection that we encounter the Lord: self-help courses can be useful in life, but to live our priestly life going from one course to another, from one method to another, leads us to become pelagians and to minimize the power of grace, which comes alive and flourishes to the extent that we, in faith, go out and give ourselves and the Gospel to others, giving what little ointment we have to those who have nothing, nothing at all" (*Homily*, Chrism Mass, 28 March 2013).

12 On this topic to which he frequently returns, the Archbishop of Buenos Aires dedicated a beautiful reflection in the homily for the Mass at the archdiocesan meeting of catechists in 2001: Cf. JM BERGOGLIO, *Lasciarsi trovare per favorire l'incontro* – Letter to catechists, March 2001, in JM BERGOGLIO – POPE FRANCIS, *È l'amore che apre gli occhi*, cit., 341-348.

13 Cf. *Ibidem*, 345.

the Year 2000 Jubilee Year[14] in his 2001 letter addressed to catechists on the feast of St Pius X, the Archbishop of Buenos Aires encouraged them to consolidate three fundamental aspects of the spiritual life of every Christian, indicating the manner and places of encounter with the Lord: an intimate and personal encounter through prayerful reading of the Word of God, the intimate and personal encounter through the Eucharist, the communal and celebratory encounter of the Sunday Mass.[15]

In his Apostolic Exhortation *EG*, Pope Francis adds that real experience of God's love in the personal encounter with Christ is the basic reason, without other lessons or instruction, which urges us to be involved in evangelization and to be 'missionary disciples'. 'Every Christian is a missionary to the extent that he or she has encountered the love of God in Christ Jesus' and it is this experience which makes them 'missionary disciples': not 'disciples' and 'missionaries', but 'missionary disciples' (*EG*, no. 120).[16] This is what happened to the first disciples (cf. Jn 1:41), to

---

14   John Paul II, *Novo Millennio Ineunte*, Apostolic Letter, 6 January 2001, in *AAS* 93 (2001), 266-309.

15   Cf. JM Bergoglio, *Lasciarsi trovare per favorire l'incontro* – Letter to catechists, March 2001, in JM BERGOGLIO – POPE FRANCIS, *È l'amore che apre gli occhi*, cit., 346-347. Concerning the places of encounter with Christ, see above: FIFTH GENERAL CONFERENCE OF THE LATIN AMERICAN AND CARIBBEAN EPISCOPATE, the *Aparecida Document*, nos 246-257.

16   We find the same idea also expressed as follows: "The primary reason for evangelizing is the love of Jesus which we have received, the experience of salvation which urges us to ever greater love of him" (*EG*, no. 264).

the Samaritan in the Gospel (Jn 4:39) and also to St Paul (Acts 9:20): they all encountered Jesus and his gaze.

The Pope then insists on the fact that by virtue of this experience, preaching is something that belongs to every Christian in day-to-day circumstances: 'Being a disciple means being constantly ready to bring the love of Jesus to others, and this can happen unexpectedly and in any place: on the street, in a city square, during work, on a journey' (*EG*, no. 127). Every Christian, then, has the duty to bring 'the fundamental message' to everyone: 'the personal love of God who became man, who gave himself up for us, who is living and who offers us his salvation and his friendship' (*EG*, no. 128).

At this point it is perhaps important to specify that the themes recalled here do not trespass on matters of an ecclesiological, missiological and spiritual nature because they also have valuable Christological merit. In Pope Francis' perspective, Christian life and missionary involvement are not simply consequences of the experience of the personal encounter with Christ in prayer, the Eucharist, the Sunday celebration, but are also 'places' and occasions for encounter and personal knowledge of Christ. Christian commitment carried out as a result of the experience of Jesus Christ and in conformity with his style are a fundamental 'Christological place' for growing in knowledge of him and for experiencing his salvation.

1.3 The faces of others

Personal encounter with Christ cannot be understood and experienced in purely ideal and intimate terms, but in a real and concrete sense. Pope Francis has often said that Christ is not an idea. He said it before being elected as Bishop of Rome[17] and often reminds us of it now.

In the prologue to his Apostolic exhortation *EG*, regarding 'the infinite love of God, who has revealed himself to us in Jesus Christ', quoting the words used in the Encyclical *Deus Caritas Est* (*DCE*), he writes: 'I never tire of repeating those words of Benedict XVI which take us to the very heart of the Gospel: "Being a Christian is not the result of an ethical choice or a lofty idea, but the encounter with an event, a person, which gives life a new horizon and a decisive direction"'[18] (*EG*, no. 7).

This is a fundamental indication for understanding the real substance of Christ for the Christian faith and the programmatic character it acquires regarding the Christian's relationship with him. It is precisely this notion, in fact, that gives rise to the awareness that today we need to overcome the danger of renouncing the 'realism of the social

---

17 "On a parallel with the paradigm of deism is the devaluation of words: words without their true weight, that do not become flesh. Words emptied of their content; at that point Christ is no longer a person but an idea. It produces an inflation of words. Ours is a nominalist culture. The word has lost its force, is empty. It lacks support, is without that 'spark' that keeps it alive and properly consists of silence" (JM BERGOGLIO, *Educare alla cultura dell'incontro* Educating to the culture of encounter – Address to the Christian Businessman's Association, September 1999, in JM BERGOGLIO – POPE FRANCIS, *È l'amore che apre gli occhi*, cit., 16).

18 Benedict XVI, *Deus Caritas Est*, Encyclical, 25 December 2005, no. 1. The same passage from Benedict XVI's Encyclical is also quoted in the Aparecida Document, cf. FIFTH GENERAL CONFERENCE OF THE LATIN AMERICAN AND CARIBBEAN EPISCOPATE, the *Aparecida Document*, no. 12.

dimension of the Gospel' and offering 'a purely spiritual Christ without flesh and without the cross' (*EG*, no. 88). The Pope says that 'the Gospel tells us constantly to run the risk of a face-to-face encounter with others, with their physical presence which challenges us, with their pain and their pleas, with their joy which infects us in our close and continuous interaction.' He then continues: 'True faith in the incarnate Son of God is inseparable from self-giving, from membership in the community, from service, from reconciliation with others. The Son of God, by becoming flesh, summoned us to the revolution of tenderness' (*EG*, no. 88).[19] Therefore, it is urgent that the Church takes up the challenge of 'respond[ing] adequately to many people's thirst for God, lest they try to satisfy it with alienating solutions or with a disembodied Jesus who demands nothing of us with regard to others' (*EG*, no. 89).

We see today's growing attraction to various forms of a '"spirituality of well-being" without community', or a '"theology of prosperity" detached from responsibility for our brothers and sisters, or to depersonalized experiences which are nothing more than a form of self-centredness' (cf. *EG*, no. 90). Instead, what is necessary is to be open to new relationships generated by Jesus Christ, including those which come to us in the form of popular religiosity[20] which

---

19 With a great sense of realism the Pope complains that "Sometimes we are tempted to be that kind of Christian who keeps the Lord's wounds at arm's length. Yet Jesus wants us to touch human misery, to touch the suffering flesh of others" (*EG*, no. 270).

20 "Expressions of popular piety have much to teach us; for those who are capable of reading them, they are a *locus theologicus*

include personal relationship with God, with Jesus Christ, with Mary, or with a Saint. There is no need to go looking for contact through vague and undefined 'harmonised energies', but we need to establish personal relationships with 'flesh' and 'faces' (cf. *EG*, no. 90). Explaining things further, the Pope adds that 'it means learning to find Jesus in the faces of others, in their voices, in their pleas. And learning to suffer in the embrace of the crucified Jesus whenever we are unjustly attacked or meet with ingratitude, never tiring of our decision to live in fraternity' (*EG*, no. 91).[21]

This indication of the concrete nature of the personal encounter with Christ in the reality of the flesh also returns in the fourth chapter of the Apostolic Exhortation, which offers four principles[22] useful for guiding our social reality and building up a people (cf. *EG*, no. 221). In his explanation of the third principle, 'Realities are more important than ideas', quoting a Scripture verse from John: 'By this you know the Spirit of God: every spirit that confesses that Jesus Christ has come in the flesh is from God' (1 Jn 4:2), the Pope links this criteria to the Incarnation of the Word of God (cf. *EG*, no. 233).

---

which demands our attention, especially at a time when we are looking to the new evangelization" (*EG*, no. 126).

21   In a note the Pope quotes the testimony of St Therese of Lisieux on interior experience concerning one Sister she found particularly disagreeable: (Ms. C, 29v-30r, in *Oeuvres Complètes*, Paris, 1992, 274-275. Cf. *EG*, no. 91, note 69.).

22   The four principles are as follows: 1) "Time is greater than space" (cf. *EG*, nos 222-225); 2) "Unity prevails over conflict" (cf. *EG*, nos 226-230); 3) "Realities are more important than ideas" (cf. *EG*, nos 231-233); 4) "The whole is greater than the part" (cf. *EG*, nos 234-237).

Furthermore, the Pope writes: 'Loving others is a spiritual force drawing us to union with God; indeed, one who does not love others "walks in the darkness" (1 Jn 2:11), "remains in death" (1 Jn 3:14) and "does not know God" (1 Jn 4:8). Benedict XVI has said that "closing our eyes to our neighbour also blinds us to God."' And then using something Benedict XVI said in *DCE*, he adds that 'closing our eyes to our neighbour also blinds us to God'[23] (*EG*, no. 272). This leads the Pope to his second conclusion: 'When we live out a spirituality of drawing nearer to others and seeking their welfare, our hearts are opened wide to the Lord's greatest and most beautiful gifts. Whenever we encounter another person in love, we learn something new about God. Whenever our eyes are opened to acknowledge the other, we grow in the light of faith and knowledge of God' (*EG*, no. 272).

Looking at the face of others is not just a social or sociological operation, nor is it merely an ecclesial or pastoral one, but it is essential for our knowledge of God and for our encounter with Christ.

2. *The 'Christological' option for the poor*

In the fourth chapter of *EG*, entitled 'The social dimension of evangelization', the Pope tackles the question of the relationship between faith and social commitment. Most of the chapter, a good thirty-one paragraphs, is dedicated to the social inclusion of the poor (nos 186-216). In his reflection, the Pope immediately clarifies things,

23 *DCE*, no. 16.

saying it is not just a social or moral argument but one of fundamental importance for faith.[24] Introducing this section he writes: 'Our faith in Christ, who became poor, and was always close to the poor and the outcast, is the basis of our concern for the integral development of society's most neglected members' (*EG*, no. 186). Thus Pope Francis specifies the Christological nature of the commitment to the liberation and promotion of the poor, which gives rise, for the Church, to 'the duty of hearing the cry of the poor' (*EG*, no. 193). The Pope quotes, in this context, a number of biblical passages from Old and New Testaments (Mt 5:7; Jas 2:12-13; Dt 4:24; Tob 12:9; Sir 3:30; 1 Pt 4:8) and, quoting a text from St Augustine,[25] also recalls the teaching of the Church Fathers on the value of giving alms, in contrast to 'the self-centred hedonism of paganism' (cf. *EG*, no. 193).

The Pope adds that no one in the Church has the right to relativize the message on behalf of the poor and that it can

---

[24] See also *EG*, no. 48: "We have to state, without mincing words, that there is an inseparable bond between our faith and the poor." See also: "The encounter with Jesus Christ in the poor is a constitutive dimension of our faith in Jesus Christ. Our option for them emerges from contemplation of his suffering face in them (Cf. Ibid. 25) and from the encounter with Him in the afflicted and outcast, whose immense dignity He himself reveals to us. It is our very adherence to Jesus Christ that makes us friends of the poor and unites us to their fate" cf. Fifth General Conference of the Latin American And Caribbean Episcopate, the *Aparecida Document*, no. 257). Cf. HM Yáñez, *L'opzione preferenziale per i poveri*, in HM Yáñez (ed.) Evangelii Gaudium: *il testo si interroga. Chiavi di lettura, testimonianze e prospettive*, Gregorian & Biblical Press, Rome 2014, 249-260.

[25] Saint Augustine, *De catechizandis rudibus*, I, XIV, 22 (PL 40, 327).

be in no way obscured or weakened (cf. *EG*, no. 194). This is as central a message to the Christian faith as is doctrine. The Pope writes: 'So why cloud something so clear? We should not be concerned simply about falling into doctrinal error, but about remaining faithful to this light-filled path of life and wisdom. For "defenders of orthodoxy are sometimes accused of passivity, indulgence, or culpable complicity regarding the intolerable situations of injustice and the political regimes which prolong them"[26]' (*EG*, no. 194).

Since the poor have a preferential place in God's heart and the whole of salvation history is marked by their presence (cf. *EG*, no. 197),[27] the option for the poor cannot be a merely cultural, sociological, political or philosophical fact for the Church, but is primarily and especially a theological category. Quoting an address by Benedict XVI,[28] the Pope points out that because of the Incarnation in poverty, the option for the poor is implicit in Christological faith. This means that the option for the poor is a preference because of its Christological nature.

Hence Francis' desire for 'a poor Church for the poor' which is capable of learning from the poor (*EG*, no. 198).[29]

---

26 The Pope quotes the CONGREGATION FOR THE DOCTRINE OF THE FAITH, *Libertatis nuntius*, Instruction, 6 August 1984, XI, no. 18, in *AAS* 76 (1984), 876-909. 907-908.

27 In *EG*, no. 197 Pope Francis quotes the following biblical passages: 2 Cor 8:9; Lk 2:24; Lev 5:7; Lk 4:18; Lk 6:20; Mt 25:35 ff.

28 BENEDICT XVI, *Address to the opening session of the 5th General Conference of the Latin American and Caribbean Episcopate*, 13 May 2007, no. 3, in *AAS* (2007), 445-460, 450.

29 Cf. also POPE FRANCIS, *Vi chiedo di pregare per me. Inizio*

Through their suffering, the poor know and allow us to know the suffering Christ. Therefore: 'We are called to find Christ in them, to lend our voice to their causes, but also to be their friends, to listen to them, to speak for them and to embrace the mysterious wisdom which God wishes to share with us through them' (*EG*, no. 198),[30] Listening to the poor and the least is way of listening to Jesus and discovering his face.

The poor, then, ought not be considered as only a pretext for condemning social, political and economic inequality, or as the beneficiaries of charity and social assistance, but as a 'theological category' which allows us to know God, see the face of Christ and understand the gospel message. This is also repeated by quoting a passage from John Paul II's Apostolic Letter NMI. Pope Francis writes: 'Without the

---

del ministero petrino di papa Francesco, Libreria Editrice Vaticana, Vatican City 2013, 21. The need for a poor Church able to listen to the poor, already expressed in the Second Vatican Council (cf. *LG*, no. 8), was taken up once more under the thrust that came from Liberation Theology, and formulated in terms of the 'preferential option for the poor' by the Latin American Episcopal Conference, especially in its plenary assemblies at Medellín in 1968 and Puebla in 1979, and again at Aparecida in 2007.

30   As Walter Kasper maintains: "The Pope's programme, a poor Church for the poor, is first of all an ecclesial, pastoral and spiritual programme' (W. KASPER, *Papa Francesco – La rivoluzione della tenerezza e dell'amore. Radici teologiche e prospettive pastorali*, Queriniana, Brescia 2015, 107. The work exists in English as *The Revolution of Tenderness and Love. Theological and Pastoral Perspectives*, Paulist Press; Translation edition, March 6, 2015). Cf. also M PAVULRAI, *Una lettura ermeneutica sul discernimento pastorale in Evangelii gaudium: le sfide e le risposte*, in HM YÁNEZ (ed.) Evangelii Gaudium: *il testo si interroga. Chiavi di lettura, testimonianze e prospettive*, Gregorian & Biblical Press, Rome 2014, 109-124.

preferential option for the poor, "the proclamation of the Gospel, which is itself the prime form of charity, risks being misunderstood or submerged by the ocean of words which daily engulfs us in today's society of mass communications"[31'] (*EG*, no. 199).

The poor and the least allow us to understand the Gospel, because Jesus, who is the 'Gospel in person', identifies with them (cf. *EG*, no. 209). So Christians are called to recognize the suffering Christ in the poor and in new forms of poverty and fragility: those who are homeless, drug-dependent, refugees, indigenous peoples, the lonely and neglected elderly, migrants, women who are marginalized and victims of ill-treatment and violence, the unborn (cf. *EG*, nos 210-213).[32]

Christian involvement thus lies at the basis of the Church which is to 'go forth' (cf. *EG*, nos 20-24): 'going forth' not to escape reality or to go to uninhabited islands, but 'to reach all the "peripheries" in need of the light of the Gospel' (*EG*, no. 20), be they geographical or existential. These are the 'places' the Church must reach out to to carry out its mission of evangelization and to encounter the Lord in the poor, the marginalized, the excluded, all those whom our 'throwaway'

---

31 *NMI*, no. 50, in *AAS* 93 (2001), 303.
32 See also JM Bergoglio, "He is not here, He is risen" - Homily, Easter Vigil 2001, in JM BERGOGLIO – POPE FRANCIS, *È l'amore che apre gli occhi*, cit., 282. "We do not walk alone in history: we are God's family. We need to look around us and with the same concern with which the women sought Jesus, seek him in the face of all our brothers and sisters living in need, loneliness, desperation."

culture reduces to being 'outcast', 'leftovers' (cf. *EG*, no. 53). In their faces and in the peripheries of humanity, Christians can see Christ, have an experience of his presence and write a new Christology.

3. The 'formalitas Christi'

Knowledge of Christ is something that comes about gradually in history for the Church and every Christian, until it reaches its fulfilment in eschatological fullness. It is growth that takes place in everyday life, beginning with the personal encounter with Christ, spending time constantly with him and being like him. This is a journey of conformation to Christ in faith and love, to be experienced in rapport with God, our neighbour and all of creation.

In his Apostolic Exhortation, Francis explains the Christian journey as one of sanctification, which matures through correspondence with God's love, and acceptance of the freely given gift of his grace (cf. *EG*, nos 161-162). He writes: 'we allow ourselves to be transformed in Christ through a life lived "according to the Spirit" (Rom 8:5)' (*EG*, no. 162),[33] thus proclaiming the gospel not only through words but especially 'by a life transfigured by God's presence' (*EG*, no. 259) and in Jesus' own style, meaning the way he treated the poor, his gestures, his consistency, his generosity and his total dedication (cf. *EG*, no. 265).[34] As Piero Coda

---

33 Cf. also *LF*, no. 21.
34 With regard to Jesus, Pope Francis writes: "… If he speaks to someone, he looks into their eyes with deep love and concern: "Jesus, looking upon him, loved him" (Mk 10:21). We

has rightly observed, it is about being transformed by Christ's gaze in order to learn to see, love, discern, speak and act with his eyes, his heart, his mind; that means that it is not just about learning Jesus' words and gestures, but learning from him.[35] It is in this sense that Christian life must be experienced as a journey of conformation to Christ which extends to the cross.

The Scriptures show us that the dimension of the cross marked the life and mission of all whom the Lord has 'chosen': Elijah (cf. 1 Kings 18:20-40; I Kings 19:4), Jonah (cf. Jon 4:1-11), Moses (cf. Ex 3:11), Isaiah (cf. Is 6:5, 7), Jeremiah (cf. Jer 1:6-8), Joseph (cf. Mt 1:19-20), John the Baptist (cf. Mt 3:14-15). In the same way, Christian life implies full and complete participation in the mission of Jesus Christ, the Son of God, as far as the cross. Bergoglio writes: 'The mission necessarily places us on the wood of the cross; this is the sign that the call received responds to the Spirit of God and not to the flesh.'[36]

Conformation of the human being to Christ occurs through acceptance of the call to mission and in its fulfilment

---

see how accessible he is, as he draws near the blind man (cf. Mk 10:46-52) and eats and drinks with sinners (cf. Mk 2:16) without worrying about being thought a glutton and a drunkard himself (cf. Mt 11:19). We see his sensitivity in allowing a sinful woman to anoint his feet (cf. Lk 7:36-50) and in receiving Nicodemus by night (cf. Jn 3:1-15). Jesus' sacrifice on the cross is nothing else than the culmination of the way he lived his entire life" (*EG, no. 269*).

35   P Coda "Oculata fides", *Leggere la realtà con gli occhi di Cristo*, in *Pontificia Academia Theologica* 12 (2014/2), 263-274, 269.

36   JM Bergoglio – Pope Francis, *Aprite la mente al vostro cuore*, cit., 56-57.

with courage and fidelity. Therefore, the response to Christ's mission implies fidelity to two fundamental and inseparable functions indicated in the Gospel account of the institution of the Twelve in Mk 3:13-19: staying with the Lord as far as the cross, and preaching. Jesus chooses his disciples and gives them the mission, not so that each of them shapes it as he wants but so that it be carried out 'according to the *formalitas Christi*.'[37]

Bergoglio says: 'The mission puts us in the same place as Jesus Christ, on the cross.'[38] The Christian is called to live his or her life in the 'from' of Christ. Two passages from John are then recalled: 'If the world hates you, be aware that it hated me before it hated you' (Jn 15:18); 'Remember the word that I said to you, 'Servants are not greater than their master.' If they persecuted me, they will persecute you; ... But they will do all these things to you on account of my name, because they do not know him who sent me' (Jn 15:20-21). He adds one further text to these: 'You did not choose me but I chose you. And I appointed you to go and bear fruit, fruit that will last' (Jn 15:16).

There is no need to come down from the cross, but there is a need to 'acquire the *formalitas Christi*', also taking on his attitudes and sentiments, as we find in the ancient Christological hymn St Paul includes in his Letter to the Philippians: 'Let the same mind be in you that was in Christ Jesus, who, though he was in the form of God, did

---

37   *Ibidem*, 59.
38   *Ivi.*

not regard equality with God as something to be exploited, but emptied himself, taking the form of a slave, being born in human likeness. And being found in human form, he humbled himself and became obedient to the point of death — even death on a cross' (Phil 2:5-8).

Christians who get involved in the mission for which they have been chosen no longer belong to themselves but have died and are risen with Christ (cf. Rom 6:3-4, 8; Col 2:12). 'The cross, then, acquires a dimension of testimony and also becomes the place we are led to when our testimony is genuine.'[39] However, the cross is not just an image that expresses the testimony of the apostle but is actually the place to which genuine testimony necessarily leads, because to accept the mission means remaining firm on the Lord's cross.

Two basic virtues are needed to remain faithful to the mission. They are strictly connected with each other and presuppose each other: courage (*parresia*) and constancy (*hypomone*). These two virtues describe the person who does not turn back but is committed to being conformed to the Lord in order to correspond to the mission he or she has received. There is a need for courage and constancy in patience in order to embrace the cross and remain on it in difficult moments, without being overcome by the temptation to come down from it, or the temptation to triumphalism. These two virtues are necessary for the apostolate because 'both come from the cross and are the

---

39 *Ibidem*, 60.

sign that the mission has been embraced with the *formalitas Christi*.'[40] We understand here that there is an intimate relationship between the Christian mission and the cross such that one cannot conceive of the mission outside the cross, not even at the foot of the cross.[41]

The process of conformation to Christ culminates in the Easter triumph which is extended to all of creation.[42] For the human being this is the ultimate fulfilment of personal and communal history. 'God's action, which began with creation whose peak was reached when he shaped man in his image and likeness – and with whom he establishes a relationship of love which reached its highest point with the Incarnation of his Son – must culminate in the full realization of this union at the universal level. The whole of creation must share in the definitive communion with God which began with the risen Christ. Therefore we are heading toward an end which is the positive conclusion of God's loving work which is not the direct result of human activity but of the Lord's saving action, the fulfilment of the work of art he himself began and which he wanted us to contribute to. The ultimate meaning of our existence is resolved, then, in the

---

40 *Ibidem*, 61.
41 *Ibidem*, 62,
42 Jesus' universal lordship is the risen and glorious one is extended to all of creation, for which, at the end of time, "the creatures of this world no longer appear to us under merely natural guise because the risen One is mysteriously holding them to himself and directing them towards fullness as their end. The very flowers of the field and the birds which his human eyes contemplated and admired are now imbued with his radiant presence" (*LS*, no. 100).

personal and communal encounter with the God who is Love, that even goes beyond death.'[43]

---

43 JM BERGOGLIO, *Educare, un impegno condiviso* (To educate, a shared task) – Message to educational communities, 2007, in JM BERGOGLIO – POPE FRANCIS, *È l'amore che apre gli occhi*, cit., 79-80. Cozzi's comment is very much to the point and substantial: "Humanity's origin in Christ is the secret of the historical and salvific process we are going through, in which the human being is transformed into a son or daughter and involved in the trinitarian embrace. Humanity's time is a time for regeneration in the image of Christ, the Son who overcame death and the old world. Dialogue with God serves precisely at realizing this transformation, bringing into being the new way of humanity's being with God which Jesus fully realized '*inconfuse et indivise*'. Being 'founded in Christ' means precisely that we inhabit this time of transfiguration during the journey of the people of God, who are the Church" (A COZZI, *La verità di Dio e dell'uomo in Cristo, Il teologico e l'antropologico nella cristologia di J. Bergoglio*, cit., 62-63).

CHAPTER 4
A WORK IN PROGRESS

The mystery of Christ is at the heart of Pope Francis' spirituality and theological perspective. Given the topics he has dealt with and the tone in which he has expressed them, and also due to the many biblical quotes and frequent references to patristic theology and earlier Magisterium, his Christology appears to have deep roots in Scripture, is in continuity with the Church's Tradition, and has been thought out and experienced in the light of the Latin American context, not given to fleeting spiritualism or abstract reductionism. As we conclude, and without entering into specific questions, it could be useful to select some of the basic features and characteristics of the Pope's Christological approach, which lie behind his teachings and gestures.

1. God's mercy and Christology

Pope Francis considers mercy to be God's fundamental attribute and the greatest of the virtues (cf. *Evangelii Gaudium*, no. 37, *EG*). This implies that mercy cannot be appreciated simply for its moral or spiritual value but must be seen above all as a useful hermeneutic principle for setting in motion a profound renewal at the theological and pastoral level. Taking mercy as a hermeneutic principle actually brings about a radical change of method, shifting from a deductive to an inductive method. This means that the departure point for theology and Christian life should not be the doctrinal principles and theological criteria traditionally used to interpret matters, but these matters themselves. In the approach indicated by Pope Francis, the historical and cultural context, and life situations, become the horizon for understanding the gospel and the demands of Christian life. This is a change of perspective which, as Cardinal Walter Kasper[1] reminds us, is something Paul VI urged on 7 December 1965 in the address he gave to the final session of the Ecumenical Council, Vatican II, through the example of the merciful Samaritan (Lk 10:25-37). By means of this parable, Jesus did not give a deductive response to the question from the doctor of the law 'Who is my neighbour?' but replied inductively, beginning with the situation of the man who had been injured and abandoned.

This approach, without diminishing the importance of theological doctrine, indicates that God and his will are known and understood not through deductive principles but through concrete life circumstances, especially in encountering the weak, the poor, the sick and the marginalized. Kasper sums up Pope Francis' deductive approach as follows: 'Your neighbour is the one you meet, who needs your help and mercy in a real situation, whom you must bend down to and whose wounds you must bind

---

1   W Kasper, *Papa Francesco – La rivoluzione della tenerezza e dell'amore*.cit., 54. *The Revolution of Tenderness and Love. Theological and Pastoral Perspectives*, Paulist Press; Translation edition, March 6, 2015.

up. He is your criterion for interpreting the concrete will of God.'[2]

The shift from a deductive to an inductive approach means that theology cannot restrict itself to analysis of the sources and interpretation of the data offered by Scripture, Tradition, the Magisterium, but must begin from the human being. Nevertheless, this is not about setting out on some kind of anthropocentric path as opposed to a theocentric one, but of taking an anthropocentric perspective determined by the Word of God and coming from theological and Christological demands.

The perspective indicated by Pope Francis becomes theologically and pastorally concrete in the '*see – judge – act*' method. Developed by Cardinal Joseph-Léon Cardijn, the founder in Belgium of the Young Christian Workers (YCW), this method was recommended by Pope John XXIII in his social Encyclical *Mater et Magistra*, 1961.[3] Then, after being widely adopted by various currents of Liberation Theology,[4] it was taken up in the General Assemblies of the Latin

---

2   *Ibidem*, 54-55.

3   Cf. POPE JOHN XXIII, *Mater et Magistra*, Encyclical, 15 May 1961, no. 236. Cf. also W. KASPER, Papa Franciesco – *La rivoluzione della tenerezza e dell'amore*, cit., 22-23.

4   Cf. P SUDAR – L GERA ET AL. (eds.) *Evangelización, liberación y reconciliación. Hacia la "Nueva evangelización"*, Ediciones Facultad de Teología de la UCS, Buenos Aires 1988; JC SCANNONE, *La filosofía de la liberación. Características, corrientes, etapas,* in *Stromata* 48 (1982), 3-40; I ELLACURÍA – J SOBRINO (eds), *Mysterium liberationis. I concetti fondamentali della teologia della liberazione*, Borla – Citadella, Rome – Assisi 1992.

American Episcopal Conference (CELAM) at Medellín (1968), Puebla (1979) and Aparecida (2007).[5]

It is a method that includes three stages for observing reality: observation or the study of problems, resources and structural conditions affecting Church and society (*see*); analysis and evaluation of real situations in the light of the Word of God, the teachings of Tradition and the Church's Magisterium (*judge*); carrying out useful interventions to resolve the problems or improve the circumstances of ecclesial and social life (*act*). From Pope Francis' perspective, it is a method which is in continuity with the Aparecida Document,[6] and is a Christological approach insofar as it sees things from Christ's point of view, judges according to Christ's teachings and acts as Christ would act.

---

[5] Cf. G WHELAN, Evangelii gaudium *come "teologia contestuale": aiutare la Chiesa ad "alzarsi al livello dei suoi tempi"*, in HM YÁNEZ (ed), Evangelii gaudium: *il testo ci interroga. Chiavi di lettura, testimonianze e prospettive*, cit., 23-38, 28-37.

[6] The Aparecida Document, drawn up by a committee over which Cardinal Jorge Mario Bergoglio presided, says: "In continuity with the previous general conferences of Latin American Bishops, this document utilizes the see-judge-act method. This method entails viewing God with the eyes of faith through his revealed word and life-giving contact with the sacraments, so that in everyday life we may see the reality around us in the light of his providence, judge it according to Jesus Christ, Way, Truth and Life, and act from the Church, the Mystical Body of Christ and universal Sacrament of salvation, in spreading the kingdom of God, which is sown on this earth and fully bears fruit in Heaven ... This method enables us to combine systematically, a faithful perspective for viewing reality; incorporating criteria from faith and reason for discerning and appraising it critically; and accordingly acting as missionary disciples of Jesus Christ" 'FIFTH GENERAL CONFERENCE OF THE LATIN AMERICAN AND CARIBBEAN EPISCOPATE, *the Aparecida Document*, no. 19.)

Such a change of theological paradigm obviously brings important consequences with it including at the pastoral and spiritual level in terms of ecclesial and personal conformation to Christ. It means that sharing in the mystery of Christ cannot be understood in any private sense, because it happens in Christian life and is only realized especially through works of spiritual and corporal works of mercy. It is on this practical level that we need to acknowledge Jesus' exhortation: 'Be merciful as your Father is merciful' (Lk 6:36). Cardinal Kasper wrote: 'Discourse on God's mercy is not, therefore, a beautiful, rhetorical but innocuous way of speaking. It does not lull us into tranquillity and illusory security; it gets us on the move; it wants our hand and especially our hearts to be open. In fact, *mercy* means having a heart for the poor, the poor taken in the broadest and most comprehensive sense.'[7] We understand that the centrality of mercy is not just an important principle at the moral or spiritual level but a decisive criterion for the renewal of theology and theological method, beginning from the human being and indeed from the poor, in strict relationship with the Church's mission.[8]

---

7   W. KASPER, Papa Francesco – *La rivoluzione della tenerezza e dell'amore*.cit., 55. Cf. also W KASPER, *Misericordia, Concetto fondamentale del vangelo*, cit., 200-219. (English: Mercy. The Essence of the Gospel and the Key to Christian Life).

8   In his Apostolic Exhortation *EG*, Pope Francis, recalling that the purpose of theology is the same as the Church's activity, appeals to theologians to carry out their service as part of the evangelizing mission of the Church. He writes. "The Church, in her commitment to evangelization, appreciates and encourages the charism of theologians and their scholarly efforts to advance

Christology must not fall into the serious trap of only developing theoretical reflection on the mystery of Christ and formulating truth 'in completely orthodox language', but must also help the Church to proclaim the kerygma, 'the heart of the Gospel', meaning 'the beauty of the saving love of God made manifest in Jesus Christ who died and rose from the dead' (*EG*, no. 36). And with regard to the language to use to communicate the truth, the Pope writes: 'There are times when the faithful, in listening to completely orthodox language, take away something alien to the authentic Gospel of Jesus Christ, because that language is alien to their own way of speaking to and understanding one another. With the holy intent of communicating the truth about God and humanity, we sometimes give them a false god or a human ideal which is not really Christian. In this way, we hold fast to a formulation while failing to convey its substance' (*EG*, no. 41).[9] This means that language does not guarantee in itself the communication of faith and truth, but that a 'completely orthodox language' could be a vehicle for 'something that does not correspond to the true Gospel of Jesus Christ.' While it might not run the risk of misunderstanding, it could risk saying that orthodoxy can sometimes be heresy, in the sense that a formally correct

dialogue with the world of cultures and sciences. I call on theologians to carry out this service as part of the Church's saving mission. In doing so, however, they must always remember that the Church and theology exist to evangelize, and not be content with a desk-bound theology" (*EG*, no. 133).

9 On the importance and nature of language, cf. also *EG*, nos 135-159.

representation of Christ put in theologically appropriate terms which does not come from a keen, real and personal knowledge, will only be partial, static and incapable of fully expressing the truth of Christ, especially the grandeur of his love and the richness of his mercy.

We can see here how Pope Francis' theological approach, marked by a strong pastoral and kerygmatic concern,[10] tends to proclamation of the Gospel and the call to conversion. It is in this spirit that he puts the emphasis on *credere in Deum* more than *credere Deum* (cf. *EG*, no. 124), that is, more on the truths to be believed, on the dynamics of Christian belief in God. In a strictly Christological sense, it seems clear that the Pope's action is not expressly focused on dogmatic truths but is pastorally addressed to proclaiming 'the Gospel of Jesus Christ' in a stimulating and fruitful manner which urges belief in and conformation to him in Christian life.

2. A pneumatic Christology

Another feature of Pope Francis' theological sensitivity concerns the pneumatic dimension of his Christological

---

10 On the relationship between theology and ministry, he keeps in mind what John Paul II wrote: "It is a question, really, of two characteristics of theology and how it is to be taught, which are not only not opposed to each other, but which work together, from different angles, in favour of a more complete "understanding of the faith." In fact the pastoral nature of theology does not mean that it should be less doctrinal or that it should be completely stripped of its scientific nature. It means, rather, that it enables future priests to proclaim the Gospel message through the cultural modes of their age and to direct pastoral action according to an authentic theological vision" (John Paul II, *Pastores Dabo Vobis*, post-synodal Apostolic Exhortation, 25 March 1992, no. 55).

thinking. He never tires of repeating that the Lord Jesus Christ who triumphed over sin and death is truly alive and acts with power. The Pope says in his Apostolic Exhortation: 'We are invited to discover this, to experience it. Christ, risen and glorified, is the wellspring of our hope, and he will not deprive us of the help we need to carry out the mission which he has entrusted to us' (*EG*, no. 275). Then he goes on, adding: 'Christ's resurrection is not an event of the past; it contains a vital power which has permeated this world. Where all seems to be dead, signs of the resurrection suddenly spring up. It is an irresistible force' (*EG*, no. 276).[11] The incarnate Son of God who died and is risen once and for all, continues to show God's mercy and show his face.

On the basis of this faith it is about noting that Christology not only concerns the person of Christ and his history, but also the 'body of Christ' that is his people. Personal and ecclesial Christian experience is a journey of conformation to Christ, by sharing in the mystery of his Incarnation and to the extent of his death and resurrection.[12] In his Encyclical on faith, Pope Francis wrote: 'Those who believe are transformed by the love to which they have opened their hearts in faith. By their openness to this offer of primordial love, their lives are enlarged and expanded. "It is

---

11 Cf. also *LS*, nos 99-100.
12 "Christ came down to earth and rose from the dead; by his Incarnation and resurrection, the Son of God embraced the whole of human life and history, and now dwells in our hearts through the Holy Spirit. Faith knows that God has drawn close to us, that Christ has been given to us as a great gift which inwardly transforms us, dwells within us and thus bestows on us the light that illumines the origin and the end of life" (*LF*, no. 20).

no longer I who live, but Christ who lives in me" (Gal 2:20). "May Christ dwell in your hearts through faith" (Eph 3:17). The self-awareness of the believer now expands because of the presence of another; it now lives in this other and thus, in love, life takes on a whole new breadth. Here we see the Holy Spirit at work. The Christian can see with the eyes of Jesus and share in his mind, his filial disposition, because he or she shares in his love, which is the Spirit. In the love of Jesus, we receive in a certain way his vision. Without being conformed to him in love, without the presence of the Spirit, it is impossible to confess him as Lord (cf. 1 Cor 12:3)' (*Lumen Fidei*, no. 21, *LF*).

The Incarnation is not only a circumscribed and particular event already carried out in the person and history of Jesus, but is also a dynamic project which, through the action of the Holy Spirit, is destined to be fulfilled in the mystery of the Church and the personal life of each human being, passing through the cross to arrive finally at the glory of risen life which is the magis of divine life.

Pope Francis' perspective thus demonstrates the features of a 'pneumatic Christology' for which, through the action of the Holy Spirit, the mystery of Christ is renewed and its mission continues in the People of God.

In the light of this, we understand that Christology is and remains a 'work in progress', always. This is not said in reference to speculative theological discussions aimed at systematizing a theoretical treatise regarding this discipline, but in order to express the Christological dynamic that marks the historical journey of the Church and of every Christian toward full conformation to Christ through the action of the Holy Spirit. Christology, inasmuch as it is an event which has already taken place in Christ and a project to be realized in the human being, is a 'work' forever in progress because it marks Christian identity and the human journey and the journey of all creation until their eschatological fulfilment.

We can also say that the experience of the faith of the People of God, enlightened by the Holy Spirit, is a fundamental hermeneutic criterion for understanding revelation and the mystery of Christ.

Pope Francis' Christological approach thus shows the merit of valuing human and ecclesial experience as a place for coming to know Christ and maturing in Christological faith.

3. An incarnate Christology

In continuity with the pneumatic dimension, a further characteristic aspect of Francis' theological sensitivity concerns the emphasis on the historical dimension of the Christ event, and especially the manner and places of his presence in history. Having matured in the Latin American theological and ecclesial context, this sensitivity leads the Pope to insist especially on the poor, who become fundamental signs for knowledge of Christ and for recognizing him.

The incarnate Son of God who died and is risen once and for all continues to manifest the mercy of God and show his face in the poor, at the peripheries of humanity, and in every gesture of love shown to one's neighbour.

This anchoring in history cannot be ignored and is underlined, because it keeps Christology far from any kind of Gnosticism and, more generally, from any outlook that empties the Incarnation of the truth of the flesh and cross of Christ. Furthermore, its object is an event realized in history and which finds the sources and coordinates in history, needed to understand, interpret and formulate it: biblical revelation, reception in Tradition, and the normative interpretation of the Magisterium.

This attention to history, however, should not be understood as an interest in facts which occurred in a distant era, or as the study of their sources. The central event of Christology, in fact, does not only concern the past of Jesus Christ's personal life which is and will always be the foundation which cannot be separated from Christian faith, but it refers also to the present in every age, to the reality of human life and the people of God on the move in this world. It is a question, then, of considering history as the theological place in which the mystery of the Incarnation of the Son of God took place and, in the flesh and the cross, where the mystery of his death and resurrection was fulfilled, but also as the theological place in which the mystery of Christ continues to manifest itself and to be fulfilled in the people of God and the life of every Christian.

This history, yesterday and today, is a fundamental 'place' for Christology because it is there that we come to knowledge of Christ through the experience of personal encounter with him and through our relationship with God, our neighbour and all of creation.

Pope Francis gives evidence of this dimension, be it through his preaching and the documents of his magisterium or by the choices and concrete gestures he has shown from the beginning of his Petrine ministry.[13] hence the embraces of babies and the sick, his preferential option for the poor, the places he has chosen for his pastoral visits.

We ought not forget that the first papal trips were to the island of Lampedusa (8 July 2013), which became a symbol of the migration emergency, and to Cagliari (22 September 2013) out of devotion to Our Lady of Bonaria, and were also made to focus attention on the suffering that comes from problems of work and unemployment. Equally significant was the opening of the Holy Door for the Extraordinary Jubilee Year of Mercy in the cathedral at Bangui, in Africa, on 29 November 2015. As Scannone says, they are all 'theological and sacramental gestures' that correspond to the theology of Pope Francis, 'a theology of the Incarnation, a theology that inculturates the faith'.[14]

So it is about a theological perspective in which the Incarnation is central in God's manifestation: an event that expresses the historical concreteness of the Christ event, but is also a paradigm for the mission entrusted to the Church, that of announcing the kerygma.[15]

13 Cf. JC SCANNONE, *Il Papa del popolo. Bergoglio raccontato dal confratello teologo gesuita e argentino*. Conversation with Bernadette Sauvaget, Libreria Editrice Vaticana, Vatican City 2015, 69.

14 *Ibidem*, 87.

15 Cf. *EG*, nos 117-118. Because of the logic of the Incarnation, Pope Francis shows the need for the inculturation of the gospel. This is about incarnating the Christian message in different cultures, such that every culture and every context re-expresses and experiences the gospel of Jesus Christ in an original and authentically salvific way. Furthermore, the Pope writes: "We cannot demand that peoples of every continent, in expressing their Christian faith, imitate modes of expression which European

nations developed at a particular moment of their history, because the faith cannot be constricted to the limits of understanding and expression of any one culture. It is an indisputable fact that no single culture can exhaust the mystery of our redemption in Christ" (*EG* 118)

www.ingramcontent.com/pod-product-compliance
Lightning Source LLC
Chambersburg PA
CBHW052027290426
44112CB00014B/2414